Penguin Monarchs

THE HOUSES OF WESSEX AND DENMARK

THE HOUSES OF NORMANDY, BLOIS AND ANJOU

THE HOUSE OF PLANTAGENET

THE HOUSES OF LANCASTER AND YORK

THE HOUSE OF TUDOR

Henry VII	Sean Cunningham
Henry VIII	John Guy
Edward VI	Stephen Alford
Mary I	John Edwards
Elizabeth I	Helen Castor

THE HOUSE OF STUART

James I	Thomas Cogswell
Charles I	Mark Kishlansky
[Cromwell	David Horspool]
Charles II	Clare Jackson
James II	David Womersley
William III & Mary II	Jonathan Keates
Anne	Richard Hewlings

THE HOUSE OF HANOVER

George I	Tim Blanning
George II	Norman Davies
George III	Amanda Foreman
George IV	Stella Tillyard
William IV	Roger Knight
Victoria	Jane Ridley

THE HOUSES OF SAXE-COBURG & GOTHA AND WINDSOR

Edward VII	Richard Davenport-Hines
George V	David Cannadine
Edward VIII	Piers Brendon
George VI	Philip Ziegler
Elizabeth II	Douglas Hurd

CARL WATKINS

Stephen
The Reign of Anarchy

ALLEN LANE
an imprint of
PENGUIN BOOKS

ALLEN LANE

UK | USA | Canada | Ireland | Australia
India | New Zealand | South Africa

Allen Lane is part of the Penguin Random House group of companies
whose addresses can be found at global.penguinrandomhouse.com.

Penguin
Random House
UK

First published 2015
001

Copyright © Carl Watkins, 2015

The moral right of the author has been asserted

Set in 9.5/13.5 pt Sabon LT Std
Typeset by Jouve (UK), Milton Keynes
Printed in Great Britain by Clays Ltd, St Ives plc

ISBN: 978-0-141-97714-0

Contents

Prologue

On the evening of 25 November 1120, ships were made ready at Barfleur, on the Normandy coast, to convey Henry I, King of England, and his son and heir, William Adelin, across the Channel. The preparations were unremarkable. Kings had regularly plied these waters. Ever since William the Conqueror's victory at Hastings had fused England and Normandy together, the king's presence in both parts of his realm had become a necessity. Henry and his son, in a customary precaution, embarked in different ships, each with large parties of courtiers. William boarded the *White Ship*.[1] New, stylish and swift, the vessel had been placed at the king's service by its captain, Thomas fitz Stephen, whose father had commanded the vessel that bore the Conqueror to England in 1066. On board, passengers and crew had broken open casks of wine; the mariners, it was later said, had, in their cups, mocked priests who came to bless the ship. 'How many of them,' wondered the monk-historian Orderic Vitalis, writing shortly after the events he described, 'had in their hearts no filial reverence for God who tempers the raging fury of wind and sea?'[2] That night the wind was still, the sea calm; stars would have pointed the way. The propitious conditions and the commonplaceness of the passage perhaps conspired with the cheering passengers, who wanted the crew to outpace the king's own ship, to make the helmsman less watchful than he would ordinarily have been. Perhaps his judgement was blurred by drink. In any event, he did not see a rock a little way outside the harbour. The ship struck it and swiftly sank. In a world where few could swim, the cries of drowning men and women carried in the cold air; they were heard on shore, and even on the king's ship, but in the darkness no one could quite make them out or discern what was happening.

Only when dawn broke did things become plain. Just one man had survived, a Rouen butcher.[3] William Adelin had very nearly got away. But, as he was being carried off to safety in a boat, he bade the rowers to turn back to save his sister, Matilda, Countess of Perche. As they did so, desperate men dragged the boat down, taking William Adelin with it.

Never, pondered the chronicler William of Malmesbury, writing in the years immediately after the sinking, had a ship brought such disaster to England.[4] With her sank not only the king's beloved son, but also his hopes and ambitions; for William Adelin was Henry I's sole legitimate male child, the future of his dynasty. The king, hearing the news of the disaster, collapsed with grief.

The chronicler traced the course of an extended tragedy in England's subsequent history thanks to the events of that night, a tragedy with its origins not only in the premature death of a prince of the blood, but also in another man's escape from the same fate: Stephen, count of the Norman county of Mortain. A younger son of Adela, daughter of William the Conqueror, Stephen was perhaps twenty-eight or twenty-nine years old in 1120. He too had been set to travel in the *White Ship*, but illness drove him ashore before she set sail.

Stephen's escape made possible a sequence of events that would, in a decade and a half, see him crowned as the fourth of England's Norman kings. Thereafter the Anglo-Norman realm would be plunged into a war that pitted him first against Henry I's daughter Matilda – whom Henry had nominated his successor following the untimely death of William Adelin – and then against Matilda's own son, Henry of Anjou. The ensuing struggle over the crown would define Stephen's rule. The Normans, whose power in Wales had waxed, found their gains mired in native rebellions; in the far north of England, the Scots king's authority displaced that of his English counterpart. Disorder consumed many other parts of England and Normandy, too, unleashed by the diminution of royal authority. All this encouraged contemporary chroniclers to depict proliferating violence, and led some modern historians to argue that, during Stephen's reign, 'anarchy' had taken hold in the realm.[5]

In November 1120, all this lay in the future. And yet William of Malmesbury, writing with hindsight, thought he saw something of history's curve in events that had unfolded since the disaster off Barfleur. William Adelin's death, Stephen's rise, and the trials and tribulations that followed, had a moral pattern and a divine purpose. These things were chastisements, punishments for the sins of king and people. But understood historically, rather than morally or theologically, Stephen's journey, from lucky escape on that November night to coronation chair fifteen years later, had nothing preordained or inexorable about it. His was a personal history saturated with contingency, formed by a concatenation of chances and mischances, the ultimate consequence of which none could have foreseen, as they looked into the future in the days after the wreck.

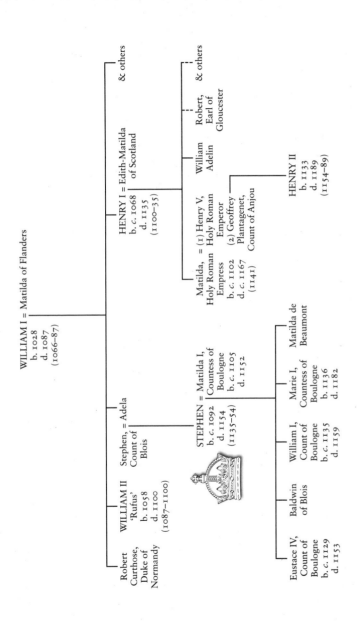

WILLIAM I = Matilda of Flanders
b. 1028
d. 1087
(1066–87)

Robert
Curthose,
Duke of
Normandy

WILLIAM II
'Rufus',
b. 1058
d. 1100
(1087–1100)

Stephen, = Adela
Count of
Blois

HENRY I = Edith-Matilda
b. c. 1068   of Scotland
d. 1135
(1100–35)

& others

STEPHEN = Matilda I,
b. c. 1092   Countess of
d. 1154   Boulogne
(1135–54)   b. c. 1105
             d. 1152

Matilda, = (1) Henry V,
Holy Roman   Holy Roman
Empress   Emperor
b. c. 1102   (2) Geoffrey
d. c. 1167   Plantagenet,
(1141)   Count of Anjou

William
Adelin

Robert,
Earl of
Gloucester

& others

Eustace IV,
Count of
Boulogne
b. c. 1129
d. 1153

Baldwin
of Blois

William I,
Count of
Boulogne
b. c. 1135
d. 1159

Marie I,
Countess of
Boulogne
b. 1136
d. 1182

Matilda de
Beaumont

HENRY II
b. 1133
d. 1189
(1154–89)

Stephen

I

Waiting for the Bomb

Henry I slipped into his final illness on the cusp of winter 1135. Only that autumn he had moved against troublemakers in southern Normandy, and in late November he paused at the castle of Lyons-la-Forêt in order to hunt, a pleasure of which he was inordinately fond. There, contrary to the advice of his physicians, he dined on lampreys. He fell ill and swiftly it became plain that there would be no recovery. Priests were fetched and barons gathered as the old king made himself right with God and man. He confessed his sins, let exiles return and allowed those he had disinherited into their lands.[1] Stephen was not there to see any of this, for he was not one of the great men who rushed to Henry's bedside. Instead, a hundred miles away in Boulogne, he was well placed to capitalize on the circumstances of his uncle's last illness. And yet the course of events he would soon seek to control was defined by the politics Henry had shaped, and by the world that William – Henry's father, Stephen's grandfather – had summoned into being when he invaded England in 1066. The story of Stephen's improbable rise begins, then, with Henry's story, with that of the Conqueror's other children and grandchildren, and with the legacies of the Conquest itself.

Henry I had made his own luck (though the chroniclers recast skill and serendipity as providence). He was the youngest of William the Conqueror's boys, and when his father died in 1087 he had received only money and no land. He had to look on as the Conqueror's second son, William Rufus, kept the eldest, Robert Curthose, out of England.[2] Normandy, the ducal family's patrimony, was long understood to be Robert's birthright, but custom allowed the Conqueror more freedom in dispensing lands acquired on the battlefield in his lifetime. That, and his estrangement from his eldest child, had encouraged him on his deathbed to send Rufus to claim England and the greater prize of a crown.[3] But then, when Rufus died suddenly in 1100, killed by a stray arrow while hunting in the New Forest, Henry saw his own chance, for Robert Curthose was far away, still on his return journey after taking the cross and joining the first crusade. Moving with similar *élan* to his predecessor, he took possession of the Treasury at Winchester and the machinery of government and claimed England for himself. The crown was his, Henry's apologists said, by right of porphyrogeniture: he had, unlike Robert, been born 'in the purple', when the Conqueror was a king rather than a mere duke – a thin skim of justification that did not conceal the reality that the crown was truly his by dint of swift action. None the less, the ill-fated Curthose had arrived in Normandy to discover his sibling already ensconced as king across the water in England, and had been unable to dislodge him. Moreover, Henry did not rest content with possession of England alone. In the years that followed, he had taken war to his brother in the duchy, and had finally defeated and captured him at the Battle of Tinchebrai in 1106. Thereafter, as his father had done, he ruled a united Anglo-Norman realm, intensifying his rule and planning to transmit the whole to his heirs, to establish a dynasty, which would be his flesh-and-blood legacy.

William Adelin had been the embodiment of his ambition. William would succeed because he was the king's eldest son, establishing that primogeniture – inheritance by the firstborn son – would in future guide the succession, reducing the chances of internecine struggle for the crown that had hitherto beset the ruling house. The king had fought to clear the path for his son. After this defeat in 1106, Robert Curthose was kept in comfortable but close confinement in Henry's castles, never to be released. His young son, William Clito, remained a menace. Roving the continent and stirring rebellion in Normandy, he was a rival-in-waiting, buoyed by the patronage of the French king, Louis the Fat, who was the duchy's feudal overlord. But Henry had attended to this, too. After he had defeated Louis at the Battle of Brémule in 1119, he forced the French king to drop his protégé's cause and to accept that William Adelin would succeed his father in Normandy. All of which meant that, as Henry boarded his own ship at Barfleur on the night of 25 November 1120, the future's course must have seemed more secure than ever.

Whatever his emotions when news of his son's drowning broke, Henry had to recover his balance swiftly. He had been a widower since the death of his queen, Edith-Matilda, in 1118. Now he remarried, choosing the youthful Adeliza of Louvain.[4] But in an ironic twist, the king, who had begotten many bastards as a younger man, could not father a child. So his hopes for the future came to turn on his daughter, Matilda, now grown into a young woman, in whom, the chronicler William of Malmesbury observed, 'lay the legitimate succession'.[5] Not only had her grandfather, uncle and father been kings, but also, through her mother, Edith-Matilda, daughter of the King of Scotland, ancient Anglo-Saxon blood-royal ran in her veins. William, the chronicler, thought he saw in her co-mingled the virtues of both parents. 'Holiness,' he said, 'found in her its equal in energy.'[6] An exalted marriage to the Holy Roman Emperor, Henry V, added to her inherited qualities. Crowned at Mainz when she was eight and marrying in 1114 at the age of twelve, she thereafter aided him in the rule of his realms. In the years after the *White Ship* sank, Matilda and her husband waited on the conception of a child, and King Henry surely looked on from England, all three envisioning the boy who might one day preside, not only over the empire, but over the Anglo-Norman realm too.

The wished-for child never came and, on 23 May 1125, that vision of the future shattered definitively: Matilda's husband the emperor died at the age of thirty-eight. Matilda returned to England. All she had to show for her German adventure was treasure and the memories that lived in her title of empress, a title she would use for the rest of her life, a residue of lost grandeur and of that bright imperial future foreclosed by her husband's untimely death. King Henry, too, had to adjust. Now, should he and Adeliza have no boy of their own, he needed to rebuild his plans for the succession more immediately around his daughter. The barons of

England and Normandy must agree to accept her as his successor, and, on 1 January 1127, Henry had them swear the oaths. Matilda would be the means, through remarriage and male children, by which a royal line might be established that would rule England and Normandy, but in the interim she might, when Henry died, have to rule in her own right.[7] The move was a bold one borne of necessity. There was no precedent near at hand for what was projected. Queens had wielded power in the name of their husbands – Edith-Matilda had done so for Henry; Matilda herself had done so for the emperor in Germany – and they might exercise authority as a regent, on behalf of a son who was not yet of age. But Henry's scheme – opening up a prospect of a queen-regnant – was an innovation in a world wedded to customs that limited such a possibility; a culture shock for an aristocracy structured by patriarchy. To enhance the chances of the scheme working, Matilda needed to marry again soon, and to bear children, to bear boys.

Matilda's eventual marriage owed much to politics outside the Anglo-Norman realm, in Flanders. The sinking of the *White Ship* had already given stimulus to the cause of Robert Curthose's son, but in 1127 it received a further dramatic boost. On 2 March, the Count of Flanders, Charles the Good, was cut down as he knelt at prayer in the Church of St Donatian in Bruges. As the moral shock of his murder spread through Christendom, King Louis of France saw an opening and, on 30 March, insinuated William Clito into the vacancy. Installed in the rich county, William was poised to menace Normandy and, in the longer term, to mount a challenge for the English crown when Henry I died: Curthose might triumph yet, vicariously, from his prison cell, or even from the grave. That Matilda herself eyed him with new apprehension is perhaps suggested in her lobbying of the king, demanding in 1126 that Curthose be moved from the castle of Cardiff to the greater security of Bristol. In any event, the new alignment of stars pointed to where Matilda must marry – Normandy's neighbour, Anjou.[8] Here the counts had long been rivals of the Norman dukes, regularly absorbed in confederations against them, but now there was cause and means for political readjustment. The means would be the marriage of Matilda to Geoffrey, son of Count Fulk. He was already handsome but, at only fifteen years of age, little more than a boy and some eleven years younger than the empress. None the less, the union would break the impending encirclement of Normandy and would, it was hoped, produce a child who would one day come into a great Anglo-Angevin inheritance. Matilda and Geoffrey were betrothed at Rouen on 22 May 1127 and marriage, amid elaborate ceremonial, followed on 17 June 1128.[9] Then, with the marriage scarcely contracted, the world turned again.

For Flanders did not fall in meekly behind its new count. William Clito had to fight for it. He had the best of the fighting, but then his luck ran out at the siege of Aalst in July. There he received a slight wound and what the chroniclers called 'St Anthony's fire' spread through his arm, which turned black and gangrenous. He died towards the end of the month.[10] The threat that the Angevin marriage was contracted to counter dissolved at once; now the domestic problems posed by the match began to come into sharper focus. For years of war had left much bad blood between Normans and Angevins, and there was a bigger difficulty too. If Henry died and Matilda succeeded as queen, who then would be the power behind the throne? Would Geoffrey rule beside her as king? Would he become, in fact if not in name, the superior partner in a hitherto untried experiment in co-rulership? It is not possible to know whether that was the cast of Henry's mind, but his actions suggest such a train of thought. The king prevaricated about the role Geoffrey might be accorded in England's governance. He also refrained from handing over castles on the Norman frontier, promised as part of Matilda's dowry, and when, in 1131, the barons' oaths to Matilda were solemnly renewed, Geoffrey was sidelined. In one crucial respect, the marriage was a striking success, for in 1133 Matilda gave her father the grandson he so desperately wanted, a baby Henry, on whose small frame now rested hopes of the dynasty's long-term survival. But the near future was filled with shadows. For the risk that the elite, the barons, would not accept Matilda could only have been strengthened by fears that, when queen, she would be bent inevitably to her husband's will. The question of the succession, whatever Henry I did, could not be settled definitively. The precedents set by the Conqueror's children in their competition over the crown, and the circle of contenders who might in future be able to stake a claim, increased the prospects of a challenge.

There were multiple imaginable futures. For if Henry had no legitimate male heir, then there were illegitimate

children, some of them boys. One, Robert, Earl of Gloucester, had been born around the end of the eleventh century
and was placed by rank, reputation and experience ahead
of the others.[11] He might be in a position to rival his
half-sister, although illegitimacy might prove an insuper-
able obstacle to his succession. There were possibilities in
the extended family, too, where the Conqueror's blood ran
in other veins – the grandsons, legitimate grandsons, of his
daughter, Adela.[12] First there was Theobald. Battle-hardened
and steady, probably in his early or mid forties, he might be
a credible claimant to the throne.

And then there was Stephen. Although Theobald's
younger brother, his material position was strong and his
political connections extensive. Henry had been unfailingly
generous, drawing him into the Anglo-Norman empire and
showering him with awards of land on both sides of the
Channel. He had been invested with the lands of Mortain in
the years after the Battle of Tinchebrai, and was granted
land in England too, including the great lordships of Eye
and Lancaster.[13] In 1125 he made a good match, marrying
the rich heiress Matilda of Boulogne, and winning with her
hand a cross-Channel portfolio of property. Henry hugged
his nephew close, favouring his young kinsman and binding
him with bonds of gratitude, making him a means to bol-
ster the Henrician order. Stephen was, the king hoped, a
man who could be counted on, a man who might make sure
that the succession happened as planned when Henry himself was in the grave. The strategy was a risk, of course.
Stephen might do contrariwise: he might unravel Henry's
scheme for his own ends. But Stephen, along with all the

other barons of the Anglo-Norman realm, had sworn the oaths to Empress Matilda, even squabbling with Robert of Gloucester about the order of precedence and about who should swear first.[14] It was a straw in the wind – an indication, perhaps, that the future would be fractious – but Stephen might at least be expected to keep a pledge that he had fought to make. The old king had done all that he could.

Henry sailed to Normandy on 2 August 1133. An earthquake tore ships' anchors from their beds, strange sounds filled the air, and a solar eclipse plunged the earth into momentary darkness.[15] So said the monk and contemporary chronicler John of Worcester. By that date, Henry was sixty-four or sixty-five years old. Few remembered a world without him. The old king had seen off one bout of illness in 1132, but all knew that the end could not be far away. Waiting for it, observed the historian R. H. C. Davis, must have been like waiting for the Bomb.[16] For when the king drew his last breath, the great edifice of authority that had been his unique creation would collapse; bonds of allegiance would break the instant life was extinct. That was the moral to be drawn from the circumstances of William the Conqueror's death. His body had been abandoned as courtiers looked to themselves and sought to defend family and property. History had repeated itself when William Rufus was struck down in the New Forest. His hunting party scattered, leaving the king's body to be borne away by peasants, 'as if it were the carcass of a slaughtered beast'.[17] Great men looked to their own defence, or to the main chance.

It was integral to the political structure that came into being in 1066 that the moment of transition between rulers was perilous precisely because Norman kings were so powerful, and because the succession was uncertain. In England the king enjoyed extraordinary authority. In the aftermath of the Conquest, William had assumed all lordship, taken all lands into his hands and re-granted them to Norman barons and ecclesiastical corporations in return for service. The landed settlement that he made limited the power of any one baron, for while William's barons received great swathes of property, this tended to be dispersed around the realm.[18] Few came to possess compact blocs of territory over which they might hold sway, which they could hope to defend with their own resources. Rather, they must look to the king to preserve their far-flung interests, defending them first against the native insurgents who struggled to reverse the Conquest, then against their peers, a sometimes predatory, conflict-prone Norman elite.

Old Henry's rule was oppressive, grasping, even brutal, but he had kept the peace. In Normandy the story was different. It remained distinct, with its own administration, but the Anglo-Norman realm was bound together by more than the person of the king. It was bound by ties of land that saw the greatest men in England holding property in Normandy as well, and by ties of emotion, to living kin, and to the bones and dust of ancestors lying in Normandy's churches.[19] The duchy was never as stable as England. Menaced from outside by powerful neighbours, threatened from within by magnates established in territories which often gave them muscle of a kind less evident over the water, its politics was more tempestuous. Henry had spent much of his time there stilling the storms. But still the king mattered, mattered very much, for great men whose interests were, inescapably, cross-Channel ones.[20]

A good deal of what came to pass in Henry I's reign, and what followed in its sequel, has to be reconstructed now from chronicles produced by churchmen.[21] Writing at a distance from events, fortified by varying degrees of hindsight, the chroniclers often distort our perceptions. Many of them saw, or thought they saw, history unfold with clarity impossible for those trapped in the moment, those men and women who were 'waiting for the Bomb'.[22] In the leaves of chronicles, thick clusterings of portents – eclipses, earthquakes, falling stars and a sort of meteorological apocalyptic (stories of tempests, floods and raging snowstorms) – evoked a world incubating turmoil during Henry's twilight years.[23] These were devices, means to conjure with dramatic tension, to show how God made known his will through signs, but the anxiety to which these passages pointed was real enough. Around the year 1135, Orderic Vitalis was grappling with prophecies of the wizard Merlin, wondering what they might mean.[24] Matilda herself was given a book of prophecy and, in the 1160s, a commentator recalled that others among the elite had shared an interest in prognostication in the years that followed Henry's death.[25]

The course of high politics explains why some minds turned in this way. From the moment the *White Ship* sank, politics was subject to constant deflections, forcing the

leading actors – the ageing king; his daughter and her husband, Geoffrey; Henry's sister, Adela, and her children; the
powerful bastard-son, Robert, Earl of Gloucester – and
then the whole cast of barons, to contemplate multiple,
competing images of the future, each itself subject to change
as events played out in the chances and mischances of indi-
vidual lives. Uncertainties about the dynasty's prospects
proved unresolvable; and they inevitably spread down-
ward, from those immediately implicated in the question of
the succession to the barons on the rungs below in the
social and political hierarchy. The temptation is to write
these men off as blood-soaked and on the make: looking
forward, perhaps, to the moment when, on Henry's death,
restraints loosened and financial demands were stilled, and
their own ambitions might be given a freer rein. And yet
these men were not – for the most part – sword-wielding
thugs. They were sharp political operators who were con-
scious that they had a great deal to lose, as well as some
things to gain if, when the king died, chaos should ensue.
There was no incentive for those who lived so well in
the Norman house to pull it down about their ears.[26] But
here lies the rub. For running under the surface of such
rational calculations were feuds with neighbours, quarrels
among kin, grievances against the dead king and his old
regime. Rationally – collectively – barons could surely see
the virtues of order, but suppressed emotions and frustrated
ambitions would have the power to generate violence when
Henry died and the king's tough love was lost.

   This much could be foreseen, for versions had played out
before, when William the Conqueror died in 1087 and,

again, when William Rufus was killed in 1100. And the fear of what might happen – not so much of the violence that might occur, but the eventual fate of the protagonists within the elite – was captured in an image of which chroniclers were fond: Fortuna, the fickle goddess, with her rotating wheel.[27] Men rose on the wheel – they won power, glory and wealth – but then, suddenly, and often inexplicably, they were dashed down, broken, penniless. For moralizing chroniclers, capricious Fortuna symbolized the instability of all things in the sublunary world. By conjuring up the image in the mind's eye, they had a moral purpose. They wanted to shift the inner gaze from the temporal to the eternal, from obsession with fame and power – the things on the wheel's rim – to the penitence and prayer that were located at its still centre. But the rhetorical trick capitalized on a world full of uncertainty, uncertainty that was deepening as the king aged and might grow further when he was gone. The barons – that status-conscious, militarized elite filled with ambition, fearful of loss, armed to the teeth but, fundamentally, grown used to Henry's controlling presence – knew that the wheel was poised to turn.

And, on 1 December 1135, it did so. In the hours of darkness, King Henry breathed his last.[28] Empress Matilda, like Stephen, was not there. She was in Anjou, caught up in the ongoing quarrel between Geoffrey and her father, and both she and her husband were entangled, too, with men Henry suspected were fermenting trouble. In the wrong place at the wrong time, Matilda was unable to make her peace with her father. Others tended to the body. This time there would be no abandonment; great men of the realm remained with the king. At the Cathedral of Rouen his bowels were drawn out so that they might be buried in Norman soil, at Notre-Dame-du-Pré; his body then waited on the abatement of contrary winds so that it might be borne back to England.[29] Fragmented in death, the king would be an abiding presence in both parts of his Anglo-Norman realm. But even as the watchers dutifully ensured the funerary script was followed, they abandoned Henry's blueprint for the succession. Robert of Gloucester, it was later claimed, was pressed to take the crown, but he was quick to rule himself out, probably sensing that, however brightly his merits burned in other respects, the Church would not set the crown on a bastard's head. Instead, he looked to Matilda's young son, Henry of Anjou.[30] Other barons looked to an adult rather than an infant, turning to Theobald of Blois, a man of middle age and a safe pair of hands in which to place the duchy and, ultimately, the crown of England.

But even as the barons in Normandy hatched their plans, they were overtaken by events across the Channel. Theobald's brother, Stephen, lost no time in setting sail from Boulogne to England when news of the king's death broke. He headed first to London, a city with trade ties to Boulogne and affection for the count.[31] There Stephen received the warmest of welcomes; he bathed in the acclamation of the people, who held him up as the new king. Stephen did not rest on these laurels, but moved swiftly on to Winchester, where the Treasury was located. Here he took possession of coin and 'vessels of gold and silver of great weight' that had been 'amassed through the enterprise of earlier kings, and most of all Henry'.[32] The author of

Gesta Stephani, a favourable account of Stephen's deeds begun during his reign and written by a churchman now unknown, noted this too: wealth from all over England had filled the coffers.[33] Now Stephen could cross palms with silver, easing with cash the consciences of reluctant converts, and buy in mercenaries, should he run into trouble. Recognition by grandees of the old regime gave him further momentum. Roger, Bishop of Salisbury, Henry's powerful minister, accepted Stephen's candidature, thus placing the sophisticated administrative machine of Norman England at Stephen's disposal, along with the men who knew how to run it. There was another important endorsement, too, or more likely a public affirmation of an agreement already made in private. Adela of Blois had another, younger, boy, Henry, who was now well placed to help Stephen's cause.[34] With little claim on family lands, Henry had entered the Church, taking vows as a Cluniac monk, but there he had risen swiftly, becoming Abbot of Glastonbury and then picking up the plum see of Winchester in 1129. Sharp-witted, educated and, thanks to his ecclesiastical postings, rich, Bishop Henry now became an eloquent voice on his brother's behalf.

By the third week of December 1135, the tide was running with the man who would be king. In Normandy, those barons who had at first looked to Theobald paused. With Stephen's cause gaining momentum in England, it might be fatal to divide the Anglo-Norman realm between the brothers, splitting the allegiances of barons who had cross-Channel interests between men who – if they conformed to the pattern set by the Conqueror's sons – might one day fall out and fight each other for the whole. Scripture itself, as the chroniclers were apt to point out, warned that a man could not serve two masters.[35] Theobald was quietly dropped.[36] Meanwhile, Matilda still, mysteriously, did nothing. She perhaps expected others to make good her claim, confident that the long-standing provisions made by her father would take effect, or she may still have been recovering from illness – a brush with death in 1134 had led her to make provision for her soul. Whatever the cause, the effect was clear: the crown was slipping out of her reach. That this was happening was not a consequence of Stephen's endeavour alone. Debate within the elite about the contenders shows that, if not Stephen, someone else would probably have squeezed Matilda out. Stephen's was a more limited kind of achievement, ensuring that, through his speed of action and singleness of purpose, fortune lighted upon him.

The preliminary steps by which Stephen seized the throne are clear, but his motives, beyond simple ambition, are hidden. He had the means to challenge. His substantial lands in England and Normandy, along with the county of Boulogne, gave him a springboard. He would have been acquainted, too, with the precedents, in 1087 and 1100, when his uncles had staged coups against a firstborn son; his early actions were almost a replica of theirs. More than that, his own family, the house of Blois, offered a recent lesson in the plasticity of inheritance, as his eldest brother, William, had been judged unfit to succeed – 'degenerate' was the blunt word of one chronicler[37] – and so the county had been passed to Theobald, the second-born boy.[38]

Stephen was also his mother's son. Through Adela, he must have learned of a glorious past: embroidery depicting the Conqueror's triumphs was said to adorn her chamber. She was sensitive to family dignity, brittle about honour, chiding her husband, the count, when he broke his crusade vows and sending him back to a martyr's death.[39] Her subsequent rule as countess-dowager – in which she defended the interests of her children with steely assurance – also showed the need for dexterity and watchfulness, for the lands of Blois were hemmed in by potentially hostile neighbours, high among them the rulers of Anjou.[40] These things so shaped Stephen that, when Henry died, he saw a chance to win fame, to emulate past glories. More than that, he must have seen danger for the house of Blois, for if Matilda came to the throne with Geoffrey by her side, his family would be vulnerable to Angevin power. Adela's boys had reason to break faith with the old king: ambition, precedent, opportunity and family strategizing all inspired Stephen's challenge.

The bold deeds of December 1135 would not, of themselves, be enough to secure the future: words, arguments, and the sanction of holy Church were necessary, too, if Stephen's rule was to be legitimized. The author of *Gesta Stephani*, writing in the middle years of the reign, reached back to its beginning to defend the basis of Stephen's kingship.[41] The crucial events had played out in London. For there, the *Gesta* author claimed, rather imaginatively, lay the right to 'elect' a new king, since the capital was the 'queen' of the kingdom. Stephen had made a grand entrance into the city. He was the object of acclamation, the chief citizens having chosen him because he was commended to them both by high birth and his personal qualities. And yet although Stephen's display of decisiveness had turned him into an unstoppable force, Matilda remained an immovable object. It was an inescapable fact that men had sworn oaths to her as Henry I's successor, and these oaths could not, contended William of Corbeil, Archbishop of Canterbury, be set aside lightly or 'in haste'. The *Gesta* author ventriloquized the words with which, he thought, Stephen's advocates persuaded the archbishop to do just this.[42] The oaths to Matilda, they said, had been forced. 'With that loud, commanding voice that none could resist', the old king, Henry I, had bent the barons to his will and so breaking a forced oath was no perjury. Moreover, on his deathbed Henry had repented of the act, so there was not even a breach with his final wishes. Here, then, were the lineaments of a case – straining at language, inventive of traditions, in places plain threadbare – that helped put the crown on Stephen's head.[43]

The heart of the matter of Stephen's rise probably lay outside these circling arguments. The chroniclers would take many different views of Stephen, but these converge in stories about violence unleashed, or in apprehensions that violence would be unleashed, in the aftermath of Henry's death.[44] In the royal forests the tight restraints of forest law had slackened, and game fell victim to a slaughter that had a ritual edge, in a time of misrule during which the king's power was in abeyance.[45] What happened there was a token of what might happen beyond the forests' bounds. In the wider world, 'the bonds of peace were torn apart'. Men fell to plunder; the strong and violent crushed the weak. 'All,' stressed John of Worcester, 'should be at peace through fear of the king, who should be as a roaring lion.'[46] If there was no king, then there would be no peace.

The *Gesta* author warmed to the same theme. Ill-fortune, he contended, fell on any country where there was no king to do justice. Moreover, the realm was filling with insurgents; a king was needed to meet them in battle, to administer the law, to restore that peace that prevailed under Henry's iron rule. There was, he said, 'no one at hand but Stephen' to do this. He was a man set on earth 'by providence' to save the kingdom in its time of danger.[47] The portrayals here were exaggerated, inflamed, and shot through with retrospection and yet they call attention, none the less, to an anxiety about proliferating disorder instinctive not only to churchmen, with their obvious stake in peace, but also to many in the lay aristocracy, men and women whose wealth and power sprang from land which would be rendered vulnerable by warfare. For such people, clergy and laity alike, it mattered very much that the 'insurgents' be met and crushed. Kingship meant so much more than war leadership in the sophisticated politics of the twelfth century, but command of men was still its irreducible core. Unspoken by the *Gesta* author – unspoken because it must have seemed so obvious it did not need to be said – was the assumption that Matilda was ill-fitted by virtue of her sex to do the things that must be done.[48] Stephen, on the other hand, was a man 'of resolution and soldierly qualities'.[49] He was battle-tested. And with the reins of power already in his hands, he was well positioned, set down as if by providence, to save the kingdom from itself.

2

A Front of Iron?

On 22 December 1135 at Westminster Abbey, William of Corbeil crowned Stephen. The ritual was invested with extraordinary imaginative power. The new king made promises – to keep the peace, to take action against evil-doers, to display justice and mercy in his judgments – and his people, both clergy and laity, acclaimed him king. He was anointed – on head, chest, shoulders, arms – before being led to the throne and given a sword. Then Archbishop William set the crown on Stephen's head. The new king was handed ring, sceptre and rod, evoking unity with his people, the power he would wield and justice he would dispense.[1] If the 'rules' of succession were uncertain, these promises and rituals were at once demonstrative and determinative. Those urging on William of Corbeil to perform the ceremony knew precisely their potency, and the *Gesta* author pictured the hesitant archbishop being pressed 'to make up, in virtue of his ministration, what seemed to have been left undone'.[2] The crowning of kings was a ritual of the profoundest depth. No amount of washing could ever remove the holy oil with which Stephen was anointed king. Ever after, this was a fact Stephen's enemies must navigate round, not a thing they could deny or reverse – the more so when, in 1136, the pope, Innocent II, gave his blessing to Stephen's election and consecration.[3] In Innocent's eyes, possession must have appeared to be nine-tenths of the law, especially where the rules of succession were inchoate and when there had been so little opposition, and to reopen the case might plunge the land into disorder.

With tremendous brio, Stephen had established himself. That this was in reality a coup, an act that overturned King Henry's wishes rather than springing from a change in them, seems beyond doubt. For while Henry's words on his deathbed cannot be recovered, it seems most unlikely, however angry the dying king might have been, that he would have chosen to shut out not only his daughter, Matilda, from the succession but also his grandson, the infant Henry, so ending at a stroke the line that he had begun, obliterating a future he had fought for so long to secure. Such perceptions could hardly have been lost on those who watched Stephen's dizzying rise. In the moment of his triumph, few were articulating in public the case against the new king, and it must have seemed as if he had pulled off a feat even more dazzling than those of Henry and William Rufus before him. But there were lessons, warnings, in the experiences of his predecessors. For having taken the crown, they had to hold on to it, to face down rebellions that broke out around them while their kingship was still fragile.

One night in his declining years, Henry I was said to have had terrible dreams. Peasants, knights and prelates took it in turns to attack him, brandishing tools, weapons and staffs. The king had sprung from his bed, scrabbling for his sword.[4] The events came to light because Grimbald, the royal physician, was said to have witnessed the scene, but its wonder for the chronicler, John of Worcester, who set it down, was that Henry – a king who, in broad daylight, was the object of terror – now, in his sleep, was terrorized himself by mere peasants. The story was artifice, the clever handiwork of a writer; but it is still a vivid evocation of how uneasily might have lain the head that wore the crown. The trick, which Henry had learned so well, was not to show it. This was what made the dreams so shocking and, from the chronicler's point of view, a tale well worth the telling: it was a revelation, a thing that none would have guessed by observing him. Stephen, too, would have to master the complementary arts of disguise and display. He would have to fashion an image for himself through the comportment he adopted and the decisions he made. By acting as a king, so he would become one. Royal power exercised effectually renewed and reproduced itself, making a king steadily stronger, as Henry I's rule had expertly demonstrated. He would need to be, or at least to appear to be, comfortable in his own majesty, to radiate the self-assurance of a man who knew, or seemed to know, that he was destined to be king. After his adroit opening, Stephen had now to begin the work of his own transformation, through image, words and deeds.

His first moves had been partially modelled on his uncle's actions. In other respects, too, he wanted to portray himself as a chip off the old block. Even before he set out for Winchester, he meted out some stern justice, making an example of plunderers by hanging some and having others set in chains.[5] But Stephen also sought to acknowledge and correct the excesses and oppressions of his predecessor's mature rule that might rankle with those whose support he now needed. At Oxford in April 1136, he issued a charter.[6] It was a brief document, framed as a promise to uphold the Church's liberties, but although in no sense a manifesto, it aimed to set the tone for the future. As these moves of his suggest, Stephen's kingship, though it might become a mighty oak full-grown, was still a fragile seedling in need of nurture. 'Almost all of the chief men,' said the *Gesta* author brightly, 'accepted [King Stephen] gladly and respectfully,' but then – in a telling qualification – he conceded that these same men had first 'received many gifts from him and likewise enlargement of their lands'.[7] This need to win men to his cause did not mark Stephen's position out as uniquely weak. Orderic Vitalis portrayed Henry I doing much the same thing as he consolidated control at the very beginning of his reign. He had 'wisely' invited the great men of the realm 'into his favour' with 'royal gifts ... adding to their loyalty'.[8] Stephen's generosity was similarly inspired and equally calculated. But generosity on such a scale had to be a passing phase: the need to shower gifts upon his barons must diminish as the reign lengthened, a reduction that served, implicitly, as a measure of the new king's strengthening authority.

Stephen's ability to assert himself within the realm that he had seized was in complex and sensitive relationship with his ability to deal with threats around its edges. For Henry's death produced not only disorders within England and Normandy, but it also triggered challenges from neighbours: from the north, where Henry's rule had seen the Scots king insinuated more deeply into English polit-ics;[9] and from the west, where Norman marchers – barons established in powerful lordships in the marches (border-lands) – had carved up the territories of the Welsh.

The Scots struck first. Their king, David I, was a younger son, a boy who, when he was born, had scant chance of ever wearing a crown.[10] Much of his early life had been spent at the court of Henry I, who had married his sister, Edith-Matilda, so binding together the ruling houses north and south of the border. In England, David had risen by virtue of the barony of Huntingdon, which was his by mar-riage, and also through the graces of the English king, which had been freely given. During his English sojourn, he also benefited from the more dubious favours of Fortuna. She whittled away his siblings so comprehensively that, in 1124, on the death of the last of his brothers, Alexander I, David succeeded to the throne of Scotland. The new king was lauded for his piety, spreading the reformed monastic life through his realm; he was, said chroniclers, a king of gentle heart. But he was also energetic and shrewd, ready to unsheath the sword to consolidate control of his Scot-tish inheritance, and modernizing its structures, applying selected lessons learned at Henry's court.[11] Down to 1135, his relations with England were shaped by friendly co-operation with his brother-in-law, but with Henry dead, the game changed. David was not only Matilda's kinsman, he had also sworn oaths in respect of the succession. Now, late in 1135 or early in 1136, he intervened in Matilda's support.

Such a noble purpose thinly camouflaged deeper ambitions

that were, for the moment at least, congruent with David's proclaimed agenda. For the question of the southern border of Scotland was not yet fixed, at least not in the estimation of its king.[12] The *Gesta* author, far in the south, envisaged a Scottish realm characterized by marshy and inhospitable terrain, filled with 'barbarous' peoples proofed by nature against the excessive cold, and defended by warriors who trusted in fleetness of foot – men who were steady in the face of death and unflinching in cruelty to their enemies.[13] But he over-defined the line between two kingdoms that, in truth, bled into each other, geographically, culturally and politically. In the west, large parts of Cumbria had been annexed only lately to England; it was William Rufus who had snuffed out the power of a regional potentate, the shadowy Dolfin, who hitherto dominated there.[14] Northumbria, too, with a historic extent that stretched across the new frontier, was incorporated more fully into England only during the reigns of Rufus and Henry, but religious affinities and landed connections still cut across the border.[15] Indeed, in some ways, Henry's reign had seen these affiliations enhanced, as new men were raised up and endowed with land in England and Scotland, acquiring a stake in both kingdoms. The Anglo-Scottish frontier was an artefact of politics rather than an expression of some profound cultural rupture.

David capitalized on this. He marched into northern England around Christmastide, testing the new regime. England's king, with all of the decisiveness that had characterized his seizure of the crown, stirred himself quickly and headed north with overwhelming forces, including mercenaries bankrolled by Henrician treasure. David was cowed into submission. Paradoxically, this early intervention worked to enhance Stephen's credibility. Negotiations followed at Durham that, on the surface, appear generous to the Scots in the terms that they yielded.[16] David agreed to withdraw from the Northumbrian territory he had seized, but in return, Prince Henry, David's son, received the lordship of Carlisle, with lands stretching into southern Cumbria. The concession was no simple pay-off; rather it was a bid to create bonds of obligation extending south of the border, renewing the stake of the Scottish king in England. As long as the balance of power was tipped firmly towards the Norman ruling house, the arrangement would help to stabilize the northern frontier.

At the same time, the ensuing Treaty of Durham – concluded on 5 February 1136 – won for Stephen recognition from a kinsman of Matilda, a powerful supporter, a man who had been poised to breathe life into the embers of her cause. A measure of Stephen's success is reflected in the actions of Robert of Gloucester. When Stephen swept to the throne, Robert had hesitated, hanging back from doing homage. But by this point it must have looked as if Stephen's coup had come off; he had faced down the Scots and may even have had word of the pope's blessing.[17] So after Easter 1136, belatedly, Robert knelt before Stephen and, placing his hands between those of the new king, made his solemn act of submission.

While David's failed invasion played out favourably for Stephen in domestic politics, the western edges of his realm were beginning to fray, however. During Henry's reign, southern Wales had been far more fully penetrated by Norman power than hitherto, much of this a consequence of private enterprise by Norman barons established in the marches.[18] Lordships had been extended, new ones carved out, castles put up and swathes of Wales colonized. But trouble was brewing in Norman Wales even before Henry was dead.[19] Gerald of Wales claimed that some of the settlers had seen all too clearly what was coming. Pools in Elfael had, he said, broken their banks, flooding the land. Flemings, meanwhile, who had colonized Rhos, had read the future using the shoulder bones of sheep – the art of scapulimancy, which they were wont to practise – and had foreseen devastation when the king's demise came.[20] Whether or not Gerald's memory served him right about the portents, that the bitter resentments built up during the decades of Norman expansion would break out after Henry's death was all too predictable, even for those unversed in such sign-reading.

On 1 January 1136, the Lord of Brycheiniog opened the Welsh account. He raised forces and met Norman troops in arms in the Gower, defeating them decisively. Bodies, it was said, went unburied, left to be scavenged by wolves; crops and churches were burned, captives made into slaves.[21] The news must have heightened anxiety in the world of the marches, but, for the moment, no more came of the insurgency. Then, in the spring, other princelings acted more decisively, triggering risings that, though unsynchronized, became widespread and sustained. Iorwerth, who ruled in Gwynllwg, Glamorgan, awaited the return of Richard fitz Gilbert de Clare, who had been King Henry's lieutenant in

Ceredigion. On 15 April, they fell on his detachment, catching the Normans unawares, and Richard was killed. More land was lost to the Normans as castles fell to princelings who swept through Ceredigion. Then, to the south, another army, of Normans and Flemings, was crushed at the Battle of Crug Mawr, near Cardigan, in October. So great was the slaughter that when the bridge across the River Tevi was broken, men crossed from bank to bank over the accumulated bodies of men and horses.[22]

By the autumn, the power of the marcher lords – and more importantly the authority of the king – in large parts of western and southern Wales was failing. The reversal was a sharp one. Henry had never been a regular presence in Wales, but the expansion of marcher power had his blessing; he made his will felt through lieutenants and, *in extremis*, he might appear in person to crush serious, confederated Welsh resistance. Stephen could not but be measured unfavourably against his predecessor, as the Welsh reversed Norman gains and Henry's erstwhile lieutenants fell to their swords. For the new king did not respond decisively. He depended on surrogates, and he dropped packets of money and mercenaries into the bottomless pit of insurgency. Eventually he gave up, leaving the Welsh to their own devices, trusting that they would fall on each other, or else reduce the land to such a state of deprivation that famine would take hold and grind the fighting to a halt.

Stephen's decisions in Wales might deal blows to royal prestige, but they were not without logic. Problems closer to home, he must have thought, called for attention.

Scattered troubles had broken out in England itself, of which one instance was serious – a rebellion fomented by Baldwin de Redvers, a baron who had steadfastly refused to do homage.[23] Instead, he now fortified Exeter against the king. The town retained its Roman walls but, more importantly, it had a strong modern castle. Stephen came in person to lay a siege, bringing up engines against it. For three months sand ran through the glass. The defenders would not yield and the king's forces could not reduce the fortifications, which comprised 'a very high mound surrounded by an impregnable wall and fortified with towers hewn of limestone'.[24] Eventually providence – so some of the chroniclers said – intervened and the springs supplying the garrison with water dried up. The defenders at first fought on, quenching flames with wine, but, with blood-drained faces and mouths gaping from thirst, they were forced to treat with the king and seek terms. Among the accounts of what followed there is a vivid set piece. The *Gesta* author portrayed Baldwin's wife pleading her husband's cause, barefoot and with her hair loose about her shoulders, a ritual of self-abasement intended to move the king to mercy. But having come to the point of breaking the siege, the king's dilemma was acute. The hard-nosed bishop Henry of Winchester told his brother to show the rebels 'a front of iron', to crush them. Other great men in Stephen's entourage, who looked to friends, to family, within the walls, counselled conciliation. The king heeded them. Acting clemently, he let Baldwin and his men march out in arms, pennants fluttering.[25] The chronicler Henry of Huntingdon, who wrote during the reign but revised his work in its wake, was unimpressed and lambasted Stephen for failing to do stern justice. He had, Henry said, taken the worst course of action in not punishing the betrayers. Had he only done so, in his view, 'there would not have been so many castles held against him later'.[26]

But Henry was reading history backwards. For Stephen, caught in the moment, the matter of what to do was poised delicately. Magnanimity might appear to be the reaction of a king who was gracious because he was strong. And mercy promised an end to rebellion without acts of incarceration or disinheritance that might prompt further unrest, and without spilling blood that might then cry out for vengeance. Moreover, both William Rufus and Henry I – neither man remembered for his forbearance – had treated rebellions early in their reigns if not quite with kid gloves, then with restrained malevolence.[27] Stephen's display of magnanimity was neither anomalous nor irrational, but the siege had been a long distraction. From May until July, it drew the gaze of the king away from other matters, troubles to which he might otherwise have given his full attention.

A place to which the king's gaze, and ultimately his person, might have travelled was Normandy. If the chroniclers are to be believed, this was one part of Stephen's realm that was in a condition of violent fermentation. Orderic Vitalis thought that the inbred bellicosity of the Norman barons had regenerated in the void that opened when Henry died. The motherland was, he said, now 'constantly in tears', and his portrayal of spreading disorder is remorselessly bleak.[28] Some of this bleakness was a matter of perspective.

To Orderic, past sixty by this point, writing an old man's book in a part of Normandy that suffered more than many of its regions in times of political dislocation, it must have seemed as if he were living in a world that was falling apart. But if Orderic's claims were over-egged, they were not unfounded. Normandy had always been more turbulent than England – especially, but not exclusively, in its border areas, and especially in those interstitial periods when one reign ended and another had barely begun.[29] Henry's pacifying presence had been regularly needed in the duchy – crushing rebellion, building castles, forging alliances – and now he was gone, many among the arms bearers had fallen readily into violence animated by ambition and score-settling. Moreover, Normandy's troubles were redoubled by the presence of Geoffrey of Anjou, husband of Matilda, poised on the frontier.

Despite the importance of Normandy, and despite the convulsions there, it was only in March 1137 that King Stephen ventured across the Channel. With money and mercenaries at his disposal, he, again, was able to put overwhelming forces into the field. Orderic was delighted. The return of a king promised the smack of firm government, the taming of the 'viper's brood' of violent men who plagued the duchy. 'The wretched people,' he said, were 'overjoyed'.[30] Stephen's campaign began well, with both diplomatic and military successes. In a diplomatic coup, Stephen arranged for his son, Eustace, to do homage to the King of France for the duchy, over which the French sovereign exercised rights as suzerain. In delegating this duty to his son, Stephen avoided abasing himself, but in orchestrating the move he also secured another recognition of his new dignity. There was initial military success for Stephen, too, when the attempted invasion of Normandy by Geoffrey of Anjou was beaten back.

And yet these inroads notwithstanding, Stephen's campaign lost momentum, and not because of any blow dealt him by an enemy but rather because of internal tensions within his own army. Mutual suspicion between the king's mercenaries, led by an able Flemish captain, William of Ypres, and native magnates from Normandy seems to have fragmented his forces. What followed was an intelligible misstep. King Henry had made wresting the duchy from the grasp of his eldest brother, Robert Curthose, his great project and one of the lessons of his mature rule was the need for watchfulness in Normandy. It must be held lest men found their allegiances divided between two rival masters. But Henry had never faced quite the kind of challenge that was now beginning to unfold on multiple fronts in England. And so, having patched things up in Normandy by way of a truce with the Angevins, Stephen decided to return thence in November, without stamping his authority on the duchy. Instead it was put into the hands of his lieutenants who, Orderic observed tartly, were now instructed by the king 'to do what he had failed to do in person'.[31]

A prominent participant in Stephen's continental venture had been Robert of Gloucester, but the relationship between the two men had deteriorated during the campaign. Stories of plots against the earl had circulated around the army and eventually he had withdrawn, entering reclusion on his estates around Caen and Bayeux. In addition to his lands in Normandy, Robert was a marcher with much property in the borderlands of Wales. He had watched as the Henrician settlement there was broken up by native enterprise and, like his peers in the marches, he had been left to fend for himself. He had responded by cutting a deal with those Welsh rulers in the south who might otherwise pose a threat.[32] Through what remained of 1137 and on into the spring of 1138, Robert did not declare his hand, watching the further disintegration of royal power in Wales and low rumblings in England. Then, as the image of Stephen's authority began to crack and splinter, a little after Whitsuntide 1138, he renounced his homage. This, suggested the earl's literary champion, William of Malmesbury, had only ever been conditional and had been given when he was in a tight spot, when all the 'chief men' had already gone over to the new king, and when even King David's challenge had been seen off.[33] Twisting and turning, William tried to form arguments that exonerated his hero from charges of breach of faith, but, whatever the justification, the implications of Robert's move were soon clear enough. The earl raised the colours of the empress; Matilda's cause was now, finally, rekindled.

Trouble in England, too, especially in the south-west where Robert was strong, was given powerful stimulus by the defection. 'It was,' said the *Gesta* author, 'like what we read of the fabled hydra of Hercules; when one head was cut off, two more grew in its place.'[34] William of Malmesbury, as hostile to the king in his weakness as he was favourable to the earl, observed that 'many [were] impelled to wrong-doing, by high birth or lofty spirit or the reckless-ness of youth'. He argued that now they 'did not hesitate to ask the king for estates or castles or . . . anything else that took their fancy', and then, if Stephen refused, 'they were at once moved to wrath, fortified castles against him, carried away great plunder from his lands'.[35] Not all of the erup-tions were conceived immediately as rebellions. Nor were they all inspired by simple quests for gain on sensing the weakness in the king. The inwardness of localized trouble was often a long-standing score that a magnate now sought to settle by way of arms. Even so, the challenge to royal power was always implicit because private wars had a pub-lic face: they showed that Stephen was unable to keep his coronation pledges. He was failing to play his part: to be the roaring lion, to guarantee the stern justice that he had promised, and that King Henry – his faults now bathed in a rose glow – had provided in abundance.

These problems could only become more acute as the claims of Matilda were steadily rejuvenated. As her for-tunes changed, consciences were pricked and some men remembered their oaths. Others, more hard-nosed, turned to her because they sought added muscle in a feud, or saw a way to lend legitimacy to a private cause by wrapping themselves in Angevin colours. Thus the particular, the localized, could become implicated in the 'national', in the very politics of succession. To Henry of Huntingdon's eye, it was as if politics were becoming unhinged as the 'abom-inable madness of traitors' reproduced itself, spreading to new places.[36] But what Henry was observing was neither simple treachery nor epidemic madness. Rather, it was a

1. Mailed knights at the charge, from an English manuscript, *c.* 1130

2. The nightmares of Henry I (from a manuscript of John of Worcester's chronicle completed during Stephen's reign): the king was said to have had terrible dreams during which he believed that, in turn, peasants, knights and (here) clergy were attacking him. Below, Henry is shown again, crossing the Channel in a scene recalling the tragedy of the *White Ship*.

3. Stephen's coronation, at the hands of William of Corbeil,
Archbishop of Canterbury, from a mid-thirteenth-century manuscript
of the *Flores Historiarum* of Matthew Paris

4. Silver coins with portraits of King William II, 'Rufus' (1087–1100),
Henry I (1100–35) and Stephen of Blois (1135–54)

5. The struggle for Lincoln in 1141, from a manuscript
of Matthew Paris's thirteenth-century *Chronica Maiora*

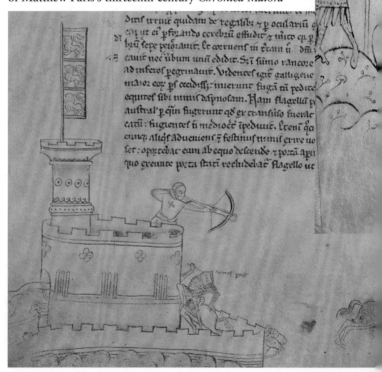

e multitudinem loricatoru equis abducit strictissime
locauit. Insules cu suis in duabus aciebus equis pug
cauros instituit. Sed admodu parue equestres acies ille
irruerunt. Paucos enim secu ficti & facciosi Insules ad
rerant. Acies autem regalis maxima erat. uno tm sa
o ipsius regis insignita uexillo. Tunc quia rex Stephs
ua carebat uoce: baldewino filio Gilleb magne nobili
scuro 7 militi fortissimo sermo exhortatori' ad uniusu cetu
unctus est.

6. The king at war: Stephen looks
on (fourth from the right), as
Baldwin fitz Gilbert rallies
his troops before the Battle
of Lincoln in 1141.

7. Empress Matilda (third from left), aged twelve, at the feast celebrating her marriage to Henry V of Germany in 1114

8. Although little stands today of the monastery of Faversham, Stephen's mausoleum, much more remains of his other foundation, Furness, in southern Cumbria, which he established in 1127 before he was king.

9. The aftermath of the siege of Shrewsbury (1138), where members of the garrison were hanged on Stephen's orders, from a manuscript of Matthew Paris's *Chronica Maiora*

10. Carvings on the west front of Lincoln Cathedral, from the time of Bishop Alexander the Magnificent (1123–48), showing souls being freed during the Harrowing of Hell, but hinting, too, at the fate of the unregenerate

11. The king at peace: in a fourteenth-century manuscript of Peter Langtoft's chronicle the king appears at leisure with a hunting falcon

concatenation of unresolved disputes, reawakened loyalties, closely observed opportunities eventuating in violent self-help, matters which were able now to flourish as the king came under challenge.

Why had this happened? Why had things gone so wrong? Henry of Huntingdon thought he had an answer. One of the king's great faults, he intimated, was that he began 'many things energetically' but then followed them up 'slothfully'.[37] Stephen saw nothing through to its end. Others concurred with Henry's remarks about restless energy, even if they abandoned his hostile tone. For Stephen's perpetual motion, as he rushed from one task to another, his propensity to leave things unfinished, was a measure of how he was now obliged to rule. Reacting, responding, stamping out brush fires when they broke out, he had little time for 'policy'. And that the Herculean enterprise now facing the king, of meeting the proliferating threats, was beyond the king's capacities is explained by the particular interaction of circumstance and character. One of the contexts for Stephen's rule was a technical challenge that would be hard for the king – for any king – to overcome. In the second quarter of the twelfth century, the balance between defensive architecture and offensive technology – between fortifications and siege machinery – was such that almost any tin-pot potentate might, for a time at least, hole up behind a castle's walls and hope to resist a prince.[38] The siege of Exeter had – in this respect, at least – been a sign of things to come. For Stephen had been resourceful in his investment of the castle, engaging slingers (from faraway lands) to harass the defenders, having engines brought up to batter the fortifications and miners brought in to bring down the walls.[39] But to no avail; he had had to settle into a lengthy siege. A reasonably modern castle, reasonably well defended, would see the king's energy break on stone.

That Stephen felt the need to be everywhere, to do everything, is entangled with the matter of how his authority, or lack of authority, was coming to be seen and, beyond that, the elusive but central issue of how he saw himself. The chronicles personalized and moralized politics, eager to show how the faults of kings, the flaws of flesh and blood, reverberated in the body politic because royal vices and virtues were punished and rewarded in history's unfolding course. 'When the head is sick,' opined Orderic, 'the whole body is afflicted; when the ruler is foolish, the whole province is in danger and the wretched people suffer utter deprivation.'[40] In the moralizing explanation is a kernel of truth. The intimacy of medieval rule – of kingship played out face to face, amid a small group of powerful men – meant that the king's personality could not but define politics. Tracing something of that personality is easier in Stephen's case because the chronicles are many and, paradoxically, because the chroniclers offered such different evaluations of the king. Polarized by the warfare between king and empress, the very partisanship of the chroniclers transforms those moments when there are echoes and resonances into meaningful convergences.

The chronicles suggest that Stephen, at least initially, attached value to the glamour of monarchy. Early in 1136 he had made a glittering progress of his realm; ritual crown-wearings subsequently allowed the king to show himself off to his subjects in all his majesty.[41] Whether Stephen was fully reconciled to the transformation wrought on him by coronation is less clear. At one remove from the throne-worthy in King Henry's day, Stephen risked being seen as a crowned magnate, a man who never quite transcended the essential tenuousness of his claim to be king. His actions betray uneasiness in his new skin; sometimes he moved unsteadily through a court that was now his own. As a count, he had won affection, eating and drinking with the humblest.[42] Now, as king, he treated men who were his barons as if they were still his peers. 'He was,' said the *Gesta* author, 'of such a kindly and gentle disposition that he commonly forgot a king's exalted rank and in many affairs saw himself not superior to his men, but in every way their equal, sometimes actually their inferior.'[43] His voice, it appears, was not quite right. Stephen's was not the loud, commanding voice of his uncle, nor the 'terrible voice' of his mighty grandfather, William I.[44] Before battle he even had to commission a magnate to address the troops on his behalf. That he was clement in handling early rebels does not distinguish him clearly from his immediate predecessors, but a number of chroniclers suggest that his rule continued to lack a hard enough edge, a certain steel.[45] It was also as if he was trapped for too long in that liminal phase, between the moment when one reign had ended and a new king came into his own, a phase when caution and measure must be the watchwords, and gifts and honours must be bestowed to bind loyalties. In that context, the uncharacteristic savagery with which he met the rebellious garrison of Shrewsbury Castle in the summer of 1138 – sending many of them to the gallows – might reveal more of the inner man. 'The unruly,' said Orderic, cheering the king on, had 'regarded his gentleness with contempt', and so it was a brutal but necessary lesson.[46] And yet there was probably more to it than that. The men had mocked the king's dignity and so – perhaps – had touched a nerve. Moreover, the relatively low estate of the rebels untied the king's hands. In truth, observers may have drawn a lesson contrary to the one Stephen intended, that this display of anger and malevolence was the exception and not the rule.

Earlier in 1138 astral flashes and spheres of fire in the heavens foretold more bloodshed and burning in the north, so the *Gesta* author suggested.[47] In February, a Scottish challenge had been seen off. 'Everywhere that the Scots attacked,' said Henry of Huntingdon, had been 'filled with horror and barbarity, accompanied by the cries of women, the wailing of the aged and the groans of the dying.' But when Stephen appeared, David had withdrawn and the English king repaid an eye for an eye, marching with fire and sword into the southern reaches of the Scottish kingdom. David 'did not dare to come to fight him'.[48] But David did not need to risk a pitched battle, which was fortunate as most of his men lacked the arms and armour of Stephen's host. Instead, he simply let the English king spend his fury and then waited on his chance, in full knowledge that the English could not stand perpetually on the defensive. Then, late in July 1138, he led his army once again out of Scotland, sweeping over the Tees, deep down into Yorkshire.

This time, detained by his troubles in the south, the king did not respond.

Into the ensuing void of leadership stepped a very improbable figure: Thurstan, Archbishop of York.[49] He was 'greatly debilitated by age' – to the point that he needed to be carried about on a litter – but he still possessed 'unyielding firmness of mind'. Thurstan applied himself to the problem at hand, the defence of the north. The northern barons, whom he had rallied, made a stand on Cowton Moor, near Northallerton, on 22 August. The force had at its heart a strange contraption – a mast strung with banners of the saints of the north, Cuthbert and Wilfrid, and a pyx containing Eucharistic wafers – which was conceived as an appeal for saintly intercession and divine protection. It gave its name to the encounter that followed, the Battle of the Standard, during which the English host inflicted a heavy defeat on King David's large but unruly army. The events of that day would be celebrated in the English chronicles as heroic, the cause as righteous, the outcome as providential. And yet under the surface was a more complex story. For if the English victory was clear, the Scots' defeat was not complete. The English knights had elected to fight on foot, and so were in no position to pursue their foes; a victory was not turned into a rout. Moreover, the decision to dismount may well have been made to rule out flight. Nerves were jittery, loyalties shaky. One powerful northern lord, Eustace fitz John – a man made by Henry I's patronage and established in a great Northumbrian barony centred on Alnwick – had fought on David's side. So too had the Cumbrians.[50] The need for an ailing Thurstan to organize the defence itself underscored a certain desperation, as did the symbolism of the standard – not only its conscription of avenging saints, but also in putting Christ's body, contained within those fragile wafers, at the heart of the army as a means to manufacture unity in the absence of the king.

So although the victory of August 1138 blunted the edge of David's ambition, it did not put an end to it. On 9 April 1139, new treaty negotiations took place at Durham. Stephen's queen, and David's niece, Matilda of Boulogne, had travelled north and woven a peace for her husband, playing the sort of role that a medieval queen might be expected to play, but also, it might be surmised, being chosen for the task because of her sharp wits and kin ties to the Scottish king. The treaty's terms disclosed that, whatever had happened on Cowton Moor the previous August, David's power was waxing and that the English king, busy in the south, was in no position to rescue the north from his embrace. David's son, Prince Henry, was confirmed in his possessions of Carlisle and Cumbria below the Solway and also in the earldom of Huntingdon. Northumbria between the Tweed and Tyne was conceded too, to be held, like David's other possessions, as fiefs of the English crown. Stephen held on to castles at Bamburgh and Newcastle. The concessions probably did little more than acknowledge that the plates of northern geopolitics had moved between December 1135 and August 1138. Northumbria had slipped out of the control of the English king. A number of barons whose interests lay primarily in the frontier region followed where Eustace fitz John had led, now seeking some kind of *modus vivendi* with the Scots king. In return for recognition of new political facts, Stephen could count – for the moment – on David and Prince Henry. In 1140, Henry would fight in Stephen's own army, honouring his obligations as a baron of the English crown, and David distanced himself from the empress, forsaking her cause.

When the *Gesta* author recalled the burning sky before the Scottish invasions, he also reflected on biblical signs, especially the story of Belshazzar, how the feasting king had watched an invisible hand writing the future on a wall.[51] The course of Stephen's reign was not nearly as firmly fixed as this rhetorical peroration implied. None the less, his position had crumbled since his early triumphs. He had swept to the throne promising, implicitly, to stifle interregnal violence and deliver stern justice, but it was becoming possible – and in parts plausible – to argue that he had done neither. In the far north, the intensification of English rule achieved by Rufus and Henry I was undone. The curious paradox was emerging that the man best placed to save the north from the 'savagery' of the men of Galloway and Lothian was their king. The Hexham historian John – writing when Stephen's reign was over but at a priory where memories of exposure to the military power of the Scots were still fresh – had praise for David.[52] And William of Newburgh, another northerner, looked back from the late twelfth century on a 'civilized king of a barbarous people'. He was a ruler whom, thanks in part to a Norman upbringing, chroniclers, and others, could separate, imaginatively, from his subjects, so sugaring the bitter pill of Scottish domination.[53]

In Wales the situation was no better. The private-enterprise expansionism of the marchers that once had been under-written by King Henry's power had turned now into frantic self-help in the face of Welsh resurgence and the new king's inaction. In England, too, and especially in the south-west, royal power weakened. When Henry of Huntingdon invented a self-justificatory speech for Robert of Gloucester, he had the earl point not only to Matilda's superior claim, the broken oaths, the 'usurpation' by Stephen, but also to failures of kingship that seemed emblematic of his inau-thenticity. For, in place of justice, Stephen had parcelled out lands 'to those who have no legal right' and so 'plundered those who are in rightful possession'. Worse, 'by throwing everything into disorder' he was 'the direct cause of the deaths of many thousands'.[54] The chronicler was armed with hindsight as well as an agenda, but he assembled a coherent argument against Stephen's kingship, elements of which were already visible in the failings of his early rule. So much of Stephen's initial appeal had been practical. His attractiveness sprang from the resolution that characterized his first moves, an earnest, it must have seemed, of effective rule to come. But by the end of 1138 it must have been possible, already, to see him in a different light.

3
Fickle Fortuna

Once Robert of Gloucester had taken up the cause of Empress Matilda there was a real prospect of an Angevin landing. Growing apprehension of that moment seems to have dictated a number of the king's actions and also to have encouraged him to take a calculated political risk. Since his advent, Stephen had leaned heavily on the structures and personnel of Henry's government.[1] He could hardly have done otherwise. He needed at hand men who could work the complex machinery and his precarious claim made it important that he effect a smooth transition, preserving at least the impression of business as usual. But now fear of Matilda's imminent arrival prompted the king to shake things up. In summer 1139, Stephen found a pretext to arrest three of the bishops appointed by Henry: Roger of Salisbury, Alexander 'the Magnificent' of Lincoln and Nigel of Ely.[2] Roger was much the most prominent of the three. He had begun his career as a priest near Caen, but was plucked from obscurity when the old king chanced upon him. Impressed by the speed at which he rattled through Mass, Henry had taken him into his service, where he became indispensible, a mainstay of administration and, ultimately, rose up to be a minister who wielded power in lieu of the king. After his arrest, he was committed to custody, initially confined in a cowshed. The sight of so worldly a prelate as Roger being pitched from the top of Fortuna's Wheel was irresistible to the chroniclers, but their delight in the moral lesson to be drawn from this was tempered by anger at the king's decision to lay hands on men of the Church.[3] That anger reverberated through ecclesiastical circles and the king's own brother, Henry, Bishop of Winchester, forced on him the humiliation of explaining himself before a legatine council.

The conundrum here is why the king was ready to risk a breach with the Church, as well as the administrative disruption the arrests might entail? Part of the answer lies in the politics of the court, for the king's judgement was, no doubt, coloured by advice from the bishops' rivals, particularly the Beaumont brothers, the powerful twins Waleran, Count of Meulan (and, after 1138, also Earl of Worcester) and Robert II, Earl of Leicester.[4] After the death of their father, Robert I, in 1118, they had been brought up at King Henry's court and now, at Stephen's right hand, they were jostling aside the leading figures of the old regime. But that is only half an explanation because, however influential the Beaumonts, the message that they poured into the king's ear must have been a potent one. The bishops, William of Malmesbury said, were men 'madly obsessed with castle-building'. They had built strong modern castles in strategically vital places, notably Bishop Roger's fortress at Devizes in Wiltshire, and because these were men who had served Matilda's father so loyally, they might well put their castles into her hands when she came.[5] The bishops had 'built castles of great renown and raised up towers and buildings of great strength, and not to put the king [Stephen] in possession of his kingdom but to steal his royal majesty'.[6]

How far the arrests of 1139 actually damaged Stephen's relationship with the Church, or broke the system of Henrician government by removing talented administrators, perhaps matters less than what the episode suggests about Stephen himself, and how the king was beginning to think.[7] For it shows him thinking tactically, ready to risk political damage for immediate military gain – and intelligibly so, as events at Exeter in 1136 could only have sharpened the king's awareness that strategically important castles must be kept out of unfriendly hands. But there is perhaps a hint here that he was more militarily astute than politically sensitive. When Walter Map, a courtier of Henry II, remembered Stephen decades later, he conceded that the former king was 'skilled in arms', but added that he was in other respects 'almost a fool'.[8] Map's pen sketch was pure caricature, but its author had fastened on to something about the king that he thought his audience would recognize. Indeed, dash, *élan* and the soldierly virtues are all conspicuous in the surviving historical evidence of Stephen's life, even that supplied by his enemies, but a lack of larger strategic calculation also emerges from the writing of contemporaries, even from those who might be counted among the king's friends.

Matilda landed on 30 September 1139 to make good her claim to the throne. Henry of Huntingdon said it was God's punishment for the arrest of the bishops, but whatever it was, it was a low-key affair. The empress arrived with Robert of Gloucester and only a small escort and travelled first to Arundel. There, as Robert slipped away to his power bases in the south-west, Matilda was entertained by another queen, King Henry's widow, Adeliza of Louvain. At Arundel, Matilda was exposed to Stephen's military power, but rather than laying a siege, he let Matilda go unimpeded and allowed her to join Earl Robert. Orderic Vitalis castigated what he saw as guileless miscalculation on the king's part. Stephen had missed a chance to 'stamp out the flames of a terrible evil that was being kindled'.[9] But the king followed a move immediate logic. For if he laid siege to the castle's massive defences, he risked a protracted engagement and reputational disaster, waging war not only on Henry's daughter, but also on the dowager queen, a woman who was, or was destined to be, married a second time to a powerful magnate, William d'Aubigny. Instead, Stephen had made a show of magnanimity and confidence in his powers; he had also behaved in an impeccable fashion, concordant with the chivalric values in which he was steeped. And for once, gender had worked in Matilda's favour.

Stephen's tactical decision at Arundel of course had a strategic price. A chronicler whose immediate field of vision extended over the troubled West Country judged that Matilda's advent 'was the beginning of despair, the most grievous – no – the ultimate, discord, bringing about the destruction of the kingdom'.[10] Baldwin de Redvers joined Matilda's cause and other prominent players in the region took her part, too. Miles of Gloucester, a potent marcher, and then Brian fitz Count, who was a man made by Henry

I, abandoned the king; the latter's castle of Wallingford, near Oxford, would now become a thorn in Stephen's flesh. By the end of 1139, and into 1140, Matilda, Robert and their backers were consolidating their positions, and violence was developing, especially around the periphery of the Angevin sphere, where it touched Stephen's England. 'There was,' Henry of Huntingdon said, 'no peace in the realm, but through murder, burning and pillage everything was being destroyed.' Everywhere there was 'the sound of war, lamentation and terror'.[11] The chronicler's claims were too sweeping, too hectic; he had extrapolated from particular horrors a general account, when, in reality, many regions were still at peace. None the less, war, civil war, was now a fact of life in south-western England, and would remain so. For while Stephen lacked the resources to drive his enemies into the sea, the Angevins were still very far from being able to topple the king.

That changed, or almost changed, in 1141. Towards the end of 1140, a crisis had blown up at Lincoln. It was relatively unremarkable. Ranulf, Earl of Chester, in confederation with his half-brother, William of Roumare, had tricked their way into Lincoln Castle and, quickly taking possession, had expelled the garrison. Ranulf was married to the daughter of Robert of Gloucester, but his quarrel with the king started narrowly, over particular claims in the castle.[12] Only subsequently did it become broader. For shortly after Christmas, and despite a peace having been agreed with Earl Ranulf, Stephen moved to recover the fortress, egged on by townsfolk who claimed to be oppressed by financial burdens visited on them by the new local regime. He hurried north and embarked upon a siege. At this point, Earl Ranulf sent to Earl Robert for help. For Robert, Ranulf's conversion to Matilda's cause, though belated, was welcome. It opened up new opportunities to apply pressure to the king. So he marched on Lincoln with the leading lights of the Angevin party, including Miles of Gloucester and Brian fitz Count. Ranulf had already slipped through the royal siege lines and so he met the rescuers en route, having also summoned up more forces of his own, among them 'wild' men from Wales who, to the horror of some of the chroniclers, were now turned loose to fight in England's intestine wars.

When the relief force came up, the king's army found itself outnumbered. There was no tactical imperative for Stephen to fight, there was time to withdraw, but, although counselled by those around him to avoid an engagement on unfavourable terms, the king none the less decided to make a stand against the rebels. As Stephen heard Mass before battle, there were worrying signs. The candle he offered shattered and the pyx chain snapped, sending eucharistic wafers tumbling to the ground.[13] The king was unmoved by the ill-omen, and on 2 February 1141, Candlemas Day, he led his army into battle against his enemies beneath the city. Baldwin fitz Gilbert, one of the king's captains and a member of the powerful Clare family, rallied Stephen's troops; Henry of Huntingdon related what he thought he might have said. The king was 'the lord's anointed' and the enemy was a motley crew. Baldwin singled the Welsh out. They would, he said, charge like cattle on to hunting spears. Robert of Gloucester, meanwhile, might give the roar of a lion but he had the heart of a rabbit.[14] The assessment was overly bright. Soon after battle was joined, the tide turned quickly against Stephen. As his forces fell back, the king found himself surrounded and overwhelmed, and although fighting bravely, he was eventually knocked down and taken prisoner. For the king defeat was a disaster; for the people of the city, it was a tragedy. Lincoln was put to the torch and its citizens slaughtered.

Stephen was taken south-westwards, first to Gloucester, then to the tight security of Earl Robert's fortress at Bristol. The fact of Stephen's kingship could not easily be over-looked, and Earl Robert, painted in his moment of triumph with customary warm hues by William of Malmesbury, had proper regard for the 'splendour of the crown', even though the king had been laid low in defeat.[15] Henry of Hunting-don made another point, giving voice to an argument Matilda's supporters were now able to set against the claim that a king, once made in the rites of coronation, could not be unmade.[16] For Henry, Lincoln was not only a military triumph and political watershed, it was the work of provi-dence, a verdict on Stephen's seizure of the crown and his subsequent rule.[17] This was the kind of argument that might help men change sides – or to explain to others, and to themselves, why they were changing sides, legitimizing the transfer of loyalties now that the king's cause seemed sud-denly, irretrievably, lost.

Matilda, meanwhile, in a reprise of Stephen's own first moves, travelled to Winchester and there took possession of the crown and the Treasury; plans for her coronation were set in motion. She was suddenly the centre of things, the subject of a massive, disruptive realignment in which men had to move, and to render account. Nowhere was intellectual and political dexterity needed more than in the case of Bishop Henry of Winchester. A little before Easter, he found himself presiding – in his capacity as papal legate – over a council convoked at Winchester.[18] During that event he made a public show of a change of heart, having already cut a deal with the Angevins behind closed doors. God, explained the bishop, had delivered a judgement on Stephen, his 'mortal brother', and so he, Henry, must yield to his 'immortal father' and accept Matilda's claims. Even the captive king appeared resigned. Thoughts of Robert Curthose's fate in Henry's prisons must have pressed in upon him, framing his expectations. Great men, the Archbishop of Canterbury among them, came to Bristol, troubled, no doubt, by their consciences, but now, with the game seemingly up, the king released them from their bonds of allegiance. With that, at a second gathering at Winchester, Matilda was presented to the political community as 'Lady of England' – a transitional style for the queen-in-waiting.[19]

But, even as the empress waited, the other Matilda, Stephen's queen, remained committed to her husband's cause and that of her son, Eustace, a boy now entering his teenage years whose eventual succession to the throne must have been her fervent hope.[20] Queen Matilda put pressure on London in support of Stephen, deploying on its outskirts forces commanded by William of Ypres. The citizens had been loyal to the king. Trade created long-standing connections between the city and Boulogne, and Stephen had actively courted the

Londoners by lightening their fiscal burdens. Their represent-
atives had held back from attending the council at which the
empress was proclaimed *Domina*, and since then she had not
striven to endear herself to the people of the city. They were
willing to be courted and cajoled by Stephen's queen. The
empress, meanwhile, did little to win friends.[21] No one could
call the Lady spendthrift. There was no showering of gifts
and honours to reward backers or appease enemies; indeed
there were confiscations and cancellations of grants made by
Stephen. There was also no relaxation of financial imposts;
quite the reverse – the empress sought to squeeze London
hard. Her manner was striking, too; there was no hint of
Stephen's informality. Rather an imperial stateliness prevailed: she was stiff and haughty. Where, wondered the *Gesta*
author, was the 'modest gait and bearing proper to the gentle
sex'?[22] When she met suppliants, she did so with a face
wrinkling into a frown, and when she spoke, it was not 'with
unassuming gentleness' but 'with a voice of authority', with
the voice of a king.

Chroniclers hostile to Stephen sometimes turned inside
out those characteristics his champions held up as virtues.
So too, we might surmise, for Matilda, though in her case
there are few partisans among the chroniclers who tried to
cast her actions in a positive light. She was, at the moment
of her triumph, the subject of a remarkable narrative
assault. The chroniclers' appreciation of her rule was
flecked by misogyny as they fumbled to make sense of the
chimera that was a queen-regnant in a world ruled by
men.[23] And yet for all the hostile reportage, her actions had
their inner logic, for they were reconstitutive of the kind of

tough love that had characterized her father's rule. They also capitalized on the imperial dignity of her past and marked a clean break with the style and substance of Stephen's reign. Of course, it was a risk for Matilda to be so hard when her position was unconsolidated. Henry's adamantine rule was a feature of his mature kingship, not his first weeks and months of power. But the risk was probably calculated. Matilda must find a way to rule as a woman, and not as a surrogate for a husband, but in her own right. If she were not hard, if she did not show a front of iron, then she would be weak, a woman who could be bent to the will of her counsellors or, worse, to that of Geoffrey of Anjou, who might turn up in England and transform himself into her ruler, and that of the country, in fact if not in name. So Matilda escaped the charge of softness and pliability – of being ruled by feminine emotions – but only to be castigated as proud and tight-fisted, headstrong and 'arbitrary'.

And yet Matilda continued to command loyalty, and that means that the chronicles have to be read against the grain of partisanship and prejudice. Matilda's fall from grace – for fall she did – was not, as the chroniclers suggested, some almost inevitable outworking of flaws in the fabric of her character, nor did it arise, at least not straightforwardly, from kingly power being trapped in a body of the 'wrong' sex. Instead, it owed much to the conditions in which she had to try to rule, and it owed more to the enterprise of that other Matilda, Stephen's queen. For the chroniclers, she was the counterpoint of the monstrous Lady.[24] She prosecuted Stephen's cause during his enforced absence with a determination that attracted none of the opprobrium visited on her namesake. This was because she wielded her husband's power in ways that were not only skilful but also familiar. Where the empress assumed an air of majestic superiority, Stephen's queen pressed for help with prayers and promises. And so, said John of Hexham, 'God frustrated the proud and gave grace to the humble'.[25] The fruits of that grace ripened on the night of 24 June 1141, the eve of the coronation, at Westminster. There, at the palace, with the tables already spread, Matilda was ready for a feast, but the Londoners had other plans. Residually loyal to Stephen, pressured by his queen and mercenary captain, William of Ypres, and squeezed by the Angevins for cash, they descended like so many buzzing bees, and Matilda and her entourage were driven out in disarray.

The empress withdrew to Oxford, where she regrouped and then travelled onwards to Winchester in July. There the wily Bishop Henry was contemplating a political reconversion.[26] After falling into dispute with the empress, and having met with Stephen's queen at Guildford, he returned to his brother's fold, finding in the idea of divine judgement he discerned in the reverses visited on the Angevins reason to take up, once again, the king's cause. When the empress Matilda arrived in Winchester, in the company of a host that included Robert of Gloucester and David of Scotland, the bishop fortified his castle against her. The events at Lincoln, earlier in the year, now played out in reverse. For Stephen's queen fell upon the town, reinforced by the resources of a major baron, Geoffrey de Mandeville, whom she had won to her side. The empress's troops, caught between the castle and Stephen's queen, faced superior forces closing in around them. The empress broke out of the encirclement and then fled, riding out at first 'male fashion', astride her horse, and then, when her nerve failed, being strapped to it, 'as if a corpse', so that she might make good her escape.[27] Others in her party, David of Scotland among them, followed the example of flight; some cast aside their armour or bartered with it to win safe passage through hostile country. Robert of Gloucester, covering the retreat, was less lucky than Matilda and David. Overwhelmed by the enemy forces, he was taken prisoner.

Robert was the empress's sword arm. He was so central to her ambitions that she could not hope to fight on without him, and so on All Saints Day 1141, Stephen's supporters, being in the ascendant, were now able to secure the release of the king for the price of Robert's freedom. Against all expectations, and after nine months of captivity, Stephen re-entered his capital. The principals were back where they had begun – or so it seemed. In practice, Matilda was gravely weakened. However harsh the criticism of her brief rule, it was still as if she had snatched defeat from the jaws of victory, and the disappointment of the reverses, in London and then Winchester, must have been shattering. Stephen's star was rising again. 'The hand of his enemies was weakened,' according to *Liber Eliensis*, a history compiled for the monks of Ely in the later twelfth century. But Stephen, too, although re-crowned at Canterbury on Christmas Day, had to contend with balances of power that had shifted. Most seriously, in Normandy, Geoffrey of

Anjou had won over men and taken much ground. On Stephen's capture, 'many', said Orderic Vitalis, 'who had previously resisted the Angevins now gave way to them'.[28] The trend in the duchy was replicated, though less fully, in the kingdom. One of the king's most important lieutenants, Waleran de Beaumont, had switched sides to the empress. His earldom of Worcester had been devised by Stephen as a bulwark against expanding Angevin power in the west, and Waleran's defection now crushed any remaining hopes of a resumption of royal authority there.

Some magnates did not change sides but, instead, simply became more autonomous. This was the development of a trend. Prior to 1141, Stephen had raised many men to the rank of earl, with perhaps some twenty-two earldoms existing in England by 1140, many of them new creations.[29] The title marked out a landholder of the highest rank, as it always had, but the rank also came to mean more in Stephen's reign than it had done hitherto. For the king invested added authority in his earls, including control of royal castles and forests and the apparatus of local government. If the king was needed in many places at once, then devolution, through delegation of responsibilities to powerful men turned royal lieutenants, offered an expedient response. The tactic, of course, came at a cost. The king's direct reach into the regions was attenuated and resources were siphoned off into private coffers. The earls, for their part, were of course only too ready to co-operate in the scheme. Avaricious old Henry had employed the sophisticated administration, with its developing court of audit, the Exchequer, to squeeze money out of the localities.[30] Now, as much of the supervisory superstructure collapsed, the barons had a chance to take control of parts of the machine for themselves. The ambitions of the earls extended beyond merely financial matters, too. They aimed at a regional intensification of magnate power, in which the reduction of royal influence would be matched by the commensurate rise of their own. But – and here is an important qualification – the purpose of these great men was not to destroy royal authority but rather to wrap themselves in it, using the strategy to shift practical power, from the king at the centre to the earl in the region.

England's coins reveal, in miniature, what was happening politically. King Henry had controlled minting savagely – mutilating moneyers he thought guilty of giving short weight – but Stephen had steadily lost control of Henry's monetary system.[31] As David consolidated his rule in the north, that region was absorbed into a Scoto-Northumbrian currency area, with coins struck using silver acquired when Cumbria was annexed and the silver mines there fell into Scottish hands. These coins came to bear David's image, or that of his son, Prince Henry, serving as tiny metallic advertisements of new authority.[32] In other parts of England that had slipped from Stephen's grasp, it was English magnates who often issued the coinage. Diversity of design and irregular dies testify to the end of central regulation, but more striking than the change is a continuity: the likeness on these issues was frequently still that of the king. Although lands, wealth and command of men gave the earls muscle, and domination of local government brought them more resources and political power, the idea that they wielded

authority in lieu of Stephen was still important. That idea –
a fiction, but a necessary one – continued to put the king's
head on most of England's varied and misshapen coins.

William of Newburgh, writing decades later, offered an
assessment of what he saw in retrospect as Stephen's failed
rule. Concentrating on the north, the region he knew best,
William depicted earls and barons who, he said, had turned
themselves into petty monarchs, each in his castle, striking
his coin, 'possessing power similar to that of a king in laying down laws for their people'.[33] These men, he claimed,
were unable to accept a superior – even an equal – and so
they came to blows, filling the land with feuds and violence.
Only the far north, where King David held sway, was peace-
able. Infused with moral assumptions, William's words
developed, implicitly, a case for the kind of strong rulership
supplied in abundance by the kings of the later twelfth century, when he was writing. None the less, with characteristic
acuity, the chronicler had put his finger on a flaw in the
design of devolved power. For however much earls wanted
to wield the king's authority in their regions, there were
circumstances in which they could not do it. The king not
only collected taxes, struck coins and defended the shores,
he also settled disputes within the ambitious and potentially fractious elite. The earls, set up in their 'countries',
could deliver some semblance of justice as they intervened
to impose settlements on lesser men (many, thought William, did what they thought to be best, though some did
what they knew to be wicked). But wherever great men
butted into others of similar rank, there was a fundamental
problem.[34] For who then would resolve their quarrels?

Even where Stephen could intervene, there was always a danger in the absence of steady royal authority that, in settling an argument in one man's favour, the other might not accept the verdict. A baron or earl discomfited by what they saw as rough justice might always seek, and more often than not find, succour elsewhere, with the Angevin party. Moreover, Stephen's earls might even struggle to impose settlements involving disputes of lesser landholders. For these men, unhappy with adjudications, might look to Matilda's supporters for help, not least because, in imitation of Stephen's strategy, Matilda was conferring earldoms on her own backers, creating a network of comital power in England to rival Stephen's own. In quarrels of these kinds, where there could be no resolution, the disputants resorted to arms. Neither Matilda nor Stephen were able to 'exercise full authority', and so, as Stephen's kingship diminished, and Matilda was unable to fill the void, in many places, in many regions, fighting broke out.[35] Once washed in blood, disputes turned into feuds filled with some of the mindless violence of which the chroniclers made so much. It was, however, violence that arose not from some innate bloodthirstiness of an arms-bearing elite, from the conduct of men whose actions were unrestrained by broader political and economic considerations or systems of moral values. Rather it sprang from a failure of kingship, and especially a failure of the royal justice to which this ambitious, fractious, land-hungry elite had become accustomed.

4
The Trackless Maze

On Christmas Day 1141, Stephen was re-crowned at Canterbury with all the panoply of lights, chanting and regalia that had attended his first coronation. It was a new beginning. And yet whatever messages were inscribed in the ritual, it seems likely that the ructions of 1141 had taken their toll on both of the chief protagonists. Matilda's nerves were shattered in the wake of the Winchester debacle, and Stephen, too, fell sick in 1142, even leading to rumours that he was dead. How far physical privations or mental pressures arising from the king's captivity brought on the collapse is unclear. But he recovered, as did the empress.

In seeking to renew her cause, Matilda now looked to her husband for help. This was a gamble, for if Geoffrey pulled the Angevin irons from the fire, then this might encourage old fears about his own ambitions. Perhaps mindful of this, but more likely too preoccupied with consolidating his control of Normandy, he did not come. He even lured Earl Robert away to the duchy to help in his campaigns there, leaving Matilda to stand, alone, on the defensive. In these circumstances, Stephen detected a military opportunity. He came up quickly to Oxford, where Matilda was lodged, trapping her inside the castle. Characteristically, the royal army was not able to take the defences by storm, and so settled instead into a siege. The noose seemed to be tightening slowly on the empress. But a little before Christmas 1142, and in the dead of night, Matilda escaped. Legend quickly crystallized around these events. With a handful of companions, so it was said, she left the castle, crossed the wintry ground 'wrapped in white garments which reflected and resembled the snow, deceiving the eyes of the besiegers', and passed over the Thames, travelling some six miles to safety.[1] The *Gesta* author wondered at the charmed life of the empress, at why God continued to preserve her.[2]

These events proved a metaphor for the politics and warfare that set in after 1141. Chance and mischance characterized these years. Matilda withdrew deeper into the West Country, where she based herself at Devizes, the great castle of Roger of Salisbury, one of the bishops arrested in 1139, and a fortress beyond Stephen's reach. The deadlock only deepened in 1143 as a move to break it on the king's part went wrong. That year, Stephen mounted a new campaign on the circumference of the Angevin sphere, circling round to Wareham, an important harbour, so as to sever communications between Angevin England and Normandy. Again, the king was unable to overcome fortifications, and so he withdrew. But now he in turn was hunted. Robert of Gloucester, who had returned from Normandy, chased him down and caught the king's army unawares, while it was encamped near Wilton Abbey.[3] The two sides came to blows on 1 July. In a messy engagement that followed, fought out partly in the dark, the king came within a whisker of capture. This time he got away, fleeing the field as a rearguard commanded by William Martel, the king's steward, kept the earl at bay. Disaster was staved off, but the price was a further erosion of the king's power in the south-west, for William was captured as he covered the retreat. The ransom of this important servant would be Sherborne Castle, one of Stephen's last remaining bastions in the region.

Having been damaged by the events at Lincoln and Winchester, neither side in the years that followed had the resources to break the other and military configurations froze hard into rigid patterns. Battlefield misadventures might have broken the deadlock, but neither Oxford nor Wilton yielded the decisive death or capture that might have ended the war by removing one of the principals. Chroniclers bore witness to the stasis in their efforts to find a framework for the narrative of these years. William of Malmesbury thought he could make sense of things down to 1141, the point at which Stephen had – providentially – fallen into the hands of his enemies, but, on the king's release, found that his history lost its shape. He was unable 'to unravel the trackless maze of events', and so, increasingly, looked to fortune as a metaphor for history's incomprehensible course.[4] The *Gesta* author understood Stephen's liberation in 1141 as a moment of redemption, but thereafter for him, too, the sequence of events lost its coherence. He spoke more of providence, looking to God for punishment of the wicked because the king could not bring it about.[5] War-weariness seeps through his prose as he tracks the ceaseless to-and-fro of combat; entries become abbreviated, fragmentary, almost as if he were losing faith in his subject.

If the battle lines came to be more deeply inscribed on the land's surface after 1141 and spheres of influence more clearly defined, it did not follow that either Stephen or Matilda were entirely secure within their regions. The authority of Earl Robert now extended from sea to sea, over almost 'half of England', but for all that power, the peace the earl, and the empress, brought in their lands was only the 'shadow of peace', it was never 'peace complete'.[6] This was, in part, because the insatiable demand for *matériel* needed to fight the war stoked resentment, but it was, more deeply, because the power of the Angevins to settle quarrels and suppress violence was uncertain, even in the regions that they notionally controlled. The king was stronger in parts where his writ ran, especially in the south-east and east of England, but his authority, too, was inevitably diminished. The Anglo-Norman realm was not simply a house divided between the rivals for the throne; within the zone controlled by each party there was further fragmentation. For, among the magnates, ties of kinship and friendship and deep vested interests in land did not respect the new lines of control. Faced by that reality, some magnates even began to disengage, wrapping themselves in 'armed neutrality', defending what they already had and augmenting it where they could.[7] Others who would not – or could not – stand back from the fighting between the contenders for the throne tacked between the parties, some-times searching for advantage, sometimes for security.

Geoffrey de Mandeville, created Earl of Essex by the king in 1140, was a man of the second type. He was too power-ful and too close to the turbulence of the 1140s to escape its effects.[8] His interests in the east of England and in London, where he held the Tower, made it impossible for him to withdraw from politics. The king and the empress both sought his support, bestowing grants and honours liberally, and so he adjusted his position repeatedly as the political geometry altered. After 1141 he was won back into the king's camp, but, not for the first time and nor for the last, rumours fermented in the court. The king could not find it in himself to trust so mercurial a figure. In 1143 Geoffrey was abruptly arrested at St Albans and forced to yield castles at Pleshey and Walden and, the greatest prize, the Tower itself, but Stephen was not willing – perhaps not able – to incarcerate the earl in perpetuity. So Geoffrey re-emerged, on parole. Uncrushed, and inveterately hostile to the king, he took to the watery fastness of the fens and began a guerrilla campaign against him. The violence that had afflicted parts of the north and the south-west of the country now had its echo in East Anglia. The temptation, then, highlighting brutality and caprice, might be to make the earl a poster boy of England's 'anarchy'.

But the story is more complicated than that. For Geoffrey de Mandeville was effectively taken prisoner twice – first by the king and then by the chroniclers who trapped the story of his life inside a morality tale. Geoffrey offered them a gift when he descended on Ramsey, Ely and Cambridge, looted ecclesiastical property and turned churches into castles.[9] When he despoiled Ramsey Abbey, its walls were said to have run red with blood that oozed from the very stone. The chroniclers drew a direct connection between Geoffrey's habit of laying sacrilegious hands on the things of holy Church and the way his rebellion ended. For, struck by an arrow at the siege of Burwell Castle in 1144, he died unshriven. Worse, as he had been excommunicated, he could not be buried, certainly not in hallowed ground. The Knights Templar took possession of his body. According to one version of what followed, they packed it into a pipe stuffed with moss, stringing it up in an orchard at their London base, the Temple Church, as they sought permission to give him Christian burial.[10] Dangling from an apple tree, twisting in the wind, Geoffrey's corpse was a warning; the story of his life was turned into an illumination of the meaningless violence that chroniclers suggested many in the elite were now busy propagating. And yet, just as Geoffrey's changes of loyalty made sense in the disturbed political world that pressed in upon him, so his behaviour in 1143 also had a logic of its own. This went beyond the evident emotional impulse to rail against a king who had humiliated him, and thereby damaged his credibility in the eyes of his peers and his men. It had a political rationale, too, to force the king into some kind of accommodation that might allow the earl to recover something of his property and his wounded honour.

What happened in the fens provided hostile chroniclers with a nice illustration of Stephen's failure. Great men disparaged the king, put up castles, ground labour and money out of the poor, oppressed the Church and showed no respect for holy things. For the Peterborough chronicler, an anonymous monk of the abbey who wrote shortly after Stephen's death, the reign's middle years supplied raw material out of which he fashioned an interpretation of the whole.

The land, he suggested, had fallen into darkness quickly when the old king died. Christ and the saints slept through long winters in which the world appeared frozen in grief and suffering.[11] For Henry of Huntingdon, the divinity was not sleeping. He was active, watchful, avenging; if the king would not punish the wicked, then God would do so, in this world and in the next, but for him, too, insensate violence fuelled by baronial ambition was the hallmark of the king's failed rule. Violence is magnified in the chronicles, fuelled by the horror churchmen felt for bloodshed that defied the Church's message of peace, and by disorder that made its institutions vulnerable. But – importantly – it was not invented. In places, where Stephen's rule had failed, disorder subsisted in the void, especially where a magnate could not introduce some semblance of authority in lieu; so, too, in the wide margins of military contact where Stephen and the Angevins faced each other, violence flared. This was not, for the most part, the senseless violence that jaundiced chroniclers sometimes made it seem. It usually had pattern and purpose. But viewed from below, a perspective we struggle to reconstruct, the suffering of the rural and urban poor who happened to be caught up in and around contested places was real enough.[12]

Stark images of misery scattered through the chronicles bear witness to something more than the anxieties of self-interested churchmen. In Worcester, as the prospect of attack loomed in 1139, townsfolk threw themselves on the mercy of its saints and refugees streamed into the cathedral church, making a lumber room of the nave with their piles of possessions. 'The cries of suckling babies and sorrowful mothers,' said John of Worcester, 'mingled with the singing of the choirs.'[13] When Hereford's turn came, the graveyard was turned over as the town's defences were hurriedly built up, the bones of ancestors poking out of the new revetments.[14] Customs, if not laws, might regulate war among the elite, but concern and quarter were less often given to the unexalted. As Earl Robert led Stephen into an honourable captivity in 1141, the people of Lincoln were put to the sword; the lintels of the cathedral's porch, built around this time, might already, by this date, have portrayed souls caught in the jaws of hell, but neither this nor similar images of divine punishment stayed the hand of the victors. Though the killing had, the *Gesta* author thought, been 'piteous' to behold, the stony-hearted Henry of Huntingdon, a local man, viewed things differently, offering a rationale for what he considered to be a not unreasonable act of war.[15]

Moreover, the eye-catching set-piece battles and occasional massacres – terrible as they were – mask everyday oppressions that arose as a consequence of the fighting.[16] Lords in their castles had to exploit land and people with a new intensity if they were to sustain their military enterprises, and marching armies had to live off the land. War itself, in which wasting – the destruction of crops, livestock and homes – was a tactic deployed in place of risky pitched battles, could mean other kinds of horror in regions where fighting raged.[17] When Stephen closed on Salisbury late in the wars, he harried that 'fair district, full of good things'. As far away as Marlborough and Devizes, houses and churches were put to the torch and, 'what was a more cruel and brutal sight', he 'fired the crops that had been reaped and stacked all over the fields'. A grim assessment: it came not from one of Stephen's antagonists, but from the pen of a supporter – the *Gesta* author, no less.[18] Just occasionally, such oppressions summoned up rage. After the Battle of Winchester, some of the high-born men of Matilda's fleeing entourage were caught and beaten by angry peasants; others had to barter their armour for their lives.[19] Such glimpses are rare, the reversals themselves surely anomalous, but they are, perhaps, brief moments when the voiceless speak, in deeds, if not in words.

Where, in the maze, was the king? In many ways he appeared to know precisely what he was doing and where he was going, working remorselessly towards achieving his chief ambitions – the security of his crown and the certainty that it would pass to his son. He retained, too, a sense of purpose in prosecuting the war: the moral he most likely extracted from those almost conclusive encounters at Lincoln, Winchester and Oxford was that a decisive blow might still be dealt on the field. But his political operations, though never without logic, continued to lack the sureness of touch that his military manoeuvres usually possessed, especially when it came to handling some of the greatest men around him. Geoffrey de Mandeville was not the only baron arrested in these years. Ranulf of Chester, even though he had re-entered the royal camp since the great rupture at Lincoln, was arrested in 1146 when the king heard whispers of perfidy. Stephen's durable gain from the drama, predictably, was some of Ranulf's castles, though at the cost of driving the earl into the arms of his enemies. It was more evidence for those who saw something of the night in the king – inconstancy, faithlessness, a suspicious nature. When Walter Map, writing in the reign of Henry II, caricatured Stephen he chose to pick out his prowess and his stupidity, but he also claimed that dim-wittedness was tinged by evil. Map played mischievously with history, yet he expected readers to recognize in his pen portrait something of the man some might still remember.[20] Of course, the contrariness Stephen displayed might have been forced by circumstance. After what happened at Lincoln, it would have been hard, for example, to rinse the bad blood out of the king's relationship with Ranulf. But the king's handling of the earl was a reprise of strategies tried before, as early as 1139; it arose from ways of regarding and treating the elite that had formed early in his rule of England. Its cause is to be found not solely in lessons that he learned from experience, but also in ways of thinking that he brought to the throne, in Stephen's sense of himself as sovereign, in the hollow ring of a man never truly reconciled to his own authority – for all the glamour of coronation and crown-wearing – shot through with suspicion of great men whose estate, he had not, in his own mind, transcended.

Increasingly, the grim equilibrium established in the early and mid 1140s was disturbed not by military victory or a political breakthrough, nor by any deliberate move of king or empress, but by a culling within the ranks of the protagonists. Innocent II, the pope who had helped to ensure that the crown lately seized remained on Stephen's head, was, in 1143, the first in a cluster of deaths and departures. Those who succeeded him on St Peter's chair would be far less favourably disposed to the king's cause.[21] Others in England and Normandy died on the battlefield or in their beds – endings sometimes picked out by chroniclers with detail about the absence of a last confession, afflictions of degenerative disease or terrifying dreams clouding the last moments, as if there was a need to find balancing punishments in this world, or indications of punishment to come in the next, to soak up all the blood that had been spilt.[22] For others there were intermissions. Waleran de Beaumont, the wily ally first of Stephen and then the empress, was one among many who heeded the call to join the Second Crusade in 1147, leaving for the Holy Land that same year to wash himself clean of sin. Then, also in 1147, there was a much more decisive ending. On the eve of All Saints' Day, Matilda was dealt a shattering setback, at once political and personal, when Robert, Earl of Gloucester fell ill with fever and died. He was, most likely, in his late fifties. After a faltering start, in which he did nothing for his half-sister, he became a most steadfast and formidable champion. He had lived at the centre of Henrician politics and brought political expertise and proven military skill to Matilda's campaign. His death might have been expected, finally, to deal a mortal blow to the Angevin cause.

But it did not. During the 1140s, the story in Normandy had been very different to that in England, with a much clearer trajectory.[23] Geoffrey of Anjou had rolled up what remained of Stephen's territory in the duchy and, in 1144, the Angevin conquest there was complete. Rouen had fallen. The new political reality had been recognized by the French king, Louis VII. So when, in 1148, Matilda decided to leave England, she was not abandoning her enterprise. After the repeated reversals and disappointments, denuded of allies, and probably robbed of all hopes of personal success, she now reinvested her ambitions in her son, the young Henry. Geoffrey had pledged to turn over the duchy to him as soon as he was of age, and they were already issuing charters in Normandy conjointly as an indication of this. The prospect of Anglo-Norman unification was renewed in a boy who was growing quickly into manhood; by 1148, it was almost time for him to make the Angevin cause his own.

5
The Shadow of the Future

As Henry grew up, Stephen must quickly have seen the shape of things to come, observing how Matilda's claim would be regenerated in this boy of the blood royal, possessed as he was of all the energy needed to take up the cause. The child had made his first visit to England in 1142, when he was just nine years old.[1] He landed at Wareham in the company of Robert of Gloucester, supplying a new figurehead for the Angevins in the wake of his mother's humiliation at London and Winchester. He had returned five years later, this time heading a small military force. The campaign he mounted was utterly inconsequential, and his mercenaries even had to be paid off by the king, perhaps in a spirit of chivalrous charity, more likely to get rid of him. It was only two years before Henry made a further visit, landing around Easter 1149.

This time he was altogether more sure-footed. At sixteen he was now on the cusp of adulthood and, with Robert of Gloucester in his grave, he was coming into his own as the leader of the Angevin cause. At Whitsuntide he passed through the warrior's rite of passage, meeting his kinsman King David, who knighted him. The encounter took place at Carlisle, the unofficial capital of the Scots king's English condominium. It was more than a moment for chivalric ritual. For Ranulf, Earl of Chester was also there and he joined the other two men to resolve their differences and to forge a common purpose. Hitherto, it is likely that little love had been lost between David and Ranulf.[2] The earl had a claim to Carlisle that reached back to the days when his father, Ranulf I, had been Henry I's man in the region. The first task of the negotiations was to patch things up, and a deal was duly brokered in which Ranulf gave up his claim but saw his rights over the honour of Lancaster confirmed in return.[3] On that basis he did homage and a confederacy was established with the territory of the English king as its target.

The meeting of 1149 marks not only the beginning of Henry's military and political coming of age, it also throws into sharp relief questions about the integrity of the kingdom Henry was fighting to win. An essential context for the Carlisle summit was the reality of Scottish power in the far north of what was, notionally, England. Neither Henry nor Ranulf of Chester could ignore this, and the circumstance was reflected in the troika's decision to mount a joint campaign focused on York. The motivations of Henry and Ranulf in this enterprise are less interesting than those of David. For he was not only projecting his power further south, into parts of northern England that he had been unable to reach, he also seems to have had York itself in his sights.[4] This plum, England's second city, meant a great deal to him not only because of its economic and strategic value, important as that was, but because its acquisition would leave him nicely placed to install a friendly archbishop, and then to extend his influence more deeply and permanently in the archdiocese. Hitherto, Scotland had had no archbishop of its own and so, in ecclesiastical matters, had been obliged to look to the ultimate authority of York. But now David might be able to equip his kingdom with its own metropolitan. It was a bold roll of the dice, by which, in one important respect, David hoped to set Scotland free.

Stephen had, substantially, spent the years since his release from captivity in the south and east of his shrunken realm, but now, sensing serious danger, he shook himself into action and marched north in a rare display of royal power beyond the Humber. It worked; the confederacy broke up.[5] And yet the most striking feature of the episode was not the failure of the compact but that it had happened at all. Implicit in the scheme hatched at Carlisle had been Henry's acknowledgement of Scottish power. The political reconfiguration of northern Britain was not simply a figment of David's far-reaching ambitions, it was a fact of political geography, and its endurance was a prospect Henry was ready to countenance, at least in the short and medium term. That readiness was, plausibly, underpinned by strategic calculations. For Henry's father had promised that he would, when he came of age, be put into possession of the duchy of Normandy. After the English adventure of 1149, Henry withdrew to the continent and there, later in the same year, his father did as he had pledged. Henry's authority in Normandy was far more important to his claim on the English throne than what might come to pass in the further reaches of what had once been northern England. For any baron in England retaining property interests in Normandy might now look to Henry, the boy growing quickly into manhood, as the one who might, in the fullness of time, bring about Anglo-Norman reunification and hope of the restoration of lost lands. Henry could afford to barter territory in the north; the duchy, however, was without price.

The prospect of undivided allegiances offered one reason for barons in England to look to a future in which Henry was king, but questions lingered about the very nature of kingship when the wars of Stephen's reign subsided. A future king might find not only that he ruled an England shorn of her northernmost territories, and, for that matter, much land that had been in Henry I's power in Wales, but also that his authority in what remained of his realm was permanently diminished. There were signs that some barons were trying to find ways to live in regions where the king's stabilizing – but potentially intrusive – presence had vanished. Some rivals began to draw back from conflict, negotiating terms with each other and sealing treaties. Two of the most powerful magnates, Robert, Earl of Leicester and Ranulf of Chester reached such an accommodation, pledging that, even if they were summoned to war by their rival lords, Stephen and Henry, each would lead no more than twenty knights into a battle that would necessarily pitch one against the other.[6] Private treaties of this kind did not, as the terms of this one spelled out, imply that the signatories would abandon their obligations to their lords, but the limitation of liabilities that they established had the potential to rob king and duke of some of their resources. More significantly, these treaties might betray a rebalancing of expectations, a tilting away from reliance on a king at centre, towards localized, communal or private means to create peace and maintain it.[7]

A deeper danger, then, for Stephen and Henry might be that, when the succession struggle ended, kingship would be reduced to a shadow of its former self. More power might come to rest in the regions, among the mightiest of the barons, who, having learned the arts of self-regulation, might prove reluctant to give up their relative independence and the financial benefits that accrued from control of royal government in the shires. But, in truth, Stephen's hasty devolution of power had produced unforeseen consequences, and these could not be so easily resolved, not even in a spirit of amity such as that which fostered the rapprochement of Robert and Ranulf. There remained the hard fact that barons seemed to need royal signs and ciphers to legitimize their newly minted authority in the regions, and there was, paradoxically, the ineluctable problem of making agreements between barons stick in the absence of that very power of the king with which the signatories to the treaties sought to dispense. All this made a reconstitution of monarchy in something like its traditional guise, rather than its emasculation, the more likely outcome when the wars eventually ended.

What this meant in practice was that a growing fraction of England's barons wanted not simply to disengage from the fighting but to oblige Stephen and Henry to come to terms. But what, exactly, might the shape of that settlement be? Neither protagonist was ready to yield. For just as Matilda's ambitions were renewed in Henry, so Stephen's claims would be carried into the future by his son, Eustace. A few years older than Henry, he had been knighted in 1147 and had since been blooded in battle. Stephen showed no sign of being ready to cut his boy out of the succession, and whatever the king might determine, there was no way that Eustace himself would quietly relinquish his rights. He had all his father's ambition for a crown, and all his zeal to fight for it. But he, and Stephen, also had a problem. Where Henry of Anjou's claim had a beautiful simplicity, resting on the fact that his grandfather's royal blood ran in his veins, that of Eustace was complicated, for his father's title depended on a combination of factors, of which much the most potent was unction – the rite that, once done, could not be undone. To smooth the way, Stephen needed to ensure that, before he himself died, the sacramental quality of his own kingship had already rubbed off on his son. To achieve this, he looked to precedents to be found not in England, but instead in France. The Capetian kings had long established the practice of anticipatory succession, of crowning an heir during the ruling monarch's lifetime, thus securing the transition. Stephen hoped to establish something similar in England.

However, a major obstacle stood in the way of Stephen realizing his ambition: the attitude of the Church.[8] By 1151, the papacy was under the influence of a new breed of reform-minded churchmen, and, thanks in large part to bitter quarrels about who should succeed Thurstan as Archbishop of York, a chill had set in between king and curia. It had spread to the relationship between Stephen and Theobald, now the Archbishop of Canterbury, who was similarly opposed to the king's plans and determined not to be the means by which bloody warfare would be resumed in the next generation.[9] When Pope Eugenius III would not give his assent to Stephen's proposals for the coronation, Theobald and his fellow bishops were implacable in their refusal to crown the king's son. So while Eustace was, in some ways, a plausible-looking king-in-waiting, Stephen's inability to have the crown set, proleptically, on the young man's head dramatically diminished the chances that he would ever wear one.

With Normandy in his hands, too, Henry's prospects were beginning to burn brighter than those of Eustace. But there were multiple delays before Henry could make anything of this. The manner of his investiture as duke had irked the French king, Louis VII, who, not having been consulted in his capacity as feudal overlord, mustered an army to demand homage with menaces. Scarcely had that threat been negotiated away than more problems surfaced for Henry, this time arising from a personal loss that had political ramifications. In September 1151 his father Geoffrey died, meaning that Henry inherited the patrimony, the lands of Anjou. Again this detained him, not least in soothing the sensitivities of brothers exercised about the settlement of family property. These events had struck just as Henry had been poised – capitalizing on his new ducal dignity – to intervene in England and so bring relief to his supporters, who were being hard pressed by the king.

That some in the elite sensed a tipping point in these years, albeit one that would not, yet, quite tip, is suggested by a curious source, a little collection of horoscopes that hint at contemporary anxieties. Astrology was an exotic, somewhat suspect and still relatively recent introduction to England from the East, but astrologers, who claimed cutting-edge knowledge that allowed them to fathom the unfathomable, to unlock political futures, might have had a certain cachet in the turbulent England of Stephen. Accordingly, the horoscopes cast in these years dwelt on the big questions. Should the king require the barons to swear oaths to his son? Would a Norman army come to England?[10]

Whatever was written in the stars, for the moment Henry did not budge from the duchy. He was delayed yet again, this time because he had decided to take a gamble. In 1152, he took the hand of Eleanor of Aquitaine.[11] She was a prize, bringing into the marriage ancestral lands, the great county of Aquitaine. The gamble came about because she was the estranged wife of Louis of France; their marriage had only very recently been dissolved. Whether or not the sudden nuptials brought on a fit of pique on the French king's part, they certainly presented him with a strategic problem in the making. He would immediately have foreseen the implications of the match for Angevin power; Henry's 'empire' was now lapping around the edges of the French kingdom, and there was an all too real possibility that Henry would soon add England to his territories, with all the resources that kingdom would put into his hands. Not only the French king was exercised by Henry's coup; Louis was able to draw together a coalition of the willing to take the fight to Henry, prominent among them Eustace, Stephen's son. The Angevin bubble seemed to be on the point of bursting, but, as his enemies massed on the Norman frontier, in the summer of 1152, Henry responded decisively, waging a lightning war in which lands of the French king were wasted, allies picked off and Louis pressured into a truce. Finally, Henry of Anjou could turn his attention to England.

Although Stephen was still firmly established, entrenched in the south-east and east of the country, his long-standing power bases, his dynastic position was crumbling. As the magnates shrank from conflict, it was becoming increasingly hard to see how the negotiations that must, one day, ensue would produce agreement that the crown should be set on Eustace's head, whether before or after Stephen's death. Even the *Gesta* author was tacking with the changing wind, for, although still loyal to Stephen, he was conceiving of a future without Eustace, a conception betrayed in recurrent references to Henry of Anjou as the king's lawful heir.[12] Moreover, as a consensus was forming about a future most likely inimical to Stephen's interests, the king suffered a terrible loss, one with profound consequences for him both personally and politically. In 1152 Matilda, his queen, died. Her death robbed the king of his most intimate and steadfast supporter and, so far as the fragments of evidence indicate, one of unusual shrewdness. The chroniclers swept laconically over her passing, and yet, without her, Stephen's struggle must have become more difficult – and more lonely.

Henry came to England again in January 1153, but this time, as he sought to bring the king to battle, the barons on both sides began to drag their feet. The two armies met first at Malmesbury, where Stephen tried to force an engagement in wintry conditions. Snowy squalls blinded the king's forces as they tried to move forward. 'God himself,' averred Henry of Huntingdon, 'seemed to be fighting on Duke Henry's side.'[13] The armies ultimately faced each other across a river swollen by rain and meltwater, unable to trade blows. Instead, a truce was formulated. Both Stephen and Henry persisted. A second encounter followed in July, this time at Wallingford. It was apt that the war should be boiled down to a struggle over this castle, for it had been a perennial problem for the king ever since Brian fitz Count, who held it, had declared for the empress. Stephen had not been able to take it, even having thrown the medieval counterpart of the kitchen sink at its fortifications.

Now, as his forces redoubled their efforts, Henry's troops mounted a counter-attack on the king's own siege castle at Crowmarsh. The stalemate was encapsulated in miniature. The main forces of both armies were now left standing off, across the Thames, but many of the leading men of each were bent on disengagement. The *Gesta* author observed that those 'of deeper judgement', on both sides, 'shrank from a conflict that was not merely between fellow countrymen but [which] meant the desolation of the whole kingdom'.[14] Henry of Huntingdon was less charitable about the motives of those involved. He depicted King Stephen and Duke Henry talking together over a stream, bemoaning the treachery in their respective ranks. The barons were unwilling to fight, said the chronicler, because they did not want to see an end to the deadlock, believing that 'if one were in fear of the other, neither would be able to exercise royal power over them'.[15] There might be just a grain of truth in Henry's mordant evaluation. Baronial motives were never unmixed. But Henry of Huntingdon was too eager to bend his analysis round one of his great preoccupations – the critique of worldliness, ambition, power – and this blinded him to the more likely calculations of the elite. The *Gesta* author, this time, was probably nearer the mark; for while some, no doubt, did indeed fear the return of strong kingship, more had perhaps learned to prefer it.

Swords were not abruptly beaten into ploughshares in the wake of the aborted battles. After so much war, the process of peace-making was slow. Mediators, men of religion, were likely to be already feeling their way to a settlement. The meeting between Stephen and Henry must have established the shape of a settlement, because Eustace quit his father's company in a rage, most plausibly because a crown that he took to be his was being bargained away. He withdrew to East Anglia, where he took out his temper on lands of the monastery of Bury St Edmunds, raiding and plundering. He fell sick and then died in August 1153, whether from grief, a convulsion, or agonies of heart, the chroniclers did not agree, but among men habitually divided in their loyalties, it is marked that there were few words of lament for him, a boy bred in war. Robbed of his wife and his eldest son in short order, something of the light seems finally to have gone out in Stephen. He made no move to reconstruct his plans for the succession around his remaining son, William, a circumstance adding to the impression that Eustace's hopes of the crown had died before he did. None the less, Eustace's death must have made it easier to bring the proposed settlement to fruition. The *Gesta* author explained that now 'it could readily be understood that God, who determines all that we do, wanted to call the duke to kingly authority and so put a stop to the interminable strife'.[16]

At a meeting in Winchester Cathedral held in November 1153, there took place a little piece of theatre vivid enough to impress the terms of the final concord on the memories of all who were present, magnates and prelates alike.[17] Stephen and Henry faced each other once again, this time separated only by the flagstones of the choir, as the terms of an agreement between them were spelled out. The core of its terms was this: Stephen would see out his days as king. He then accepted Henry of Anjou as his heir, and the king's surviving son, William, would be rewarded generously with property as compensation for being cut out of the succession. That was a token of how a broader settlement would pan out when Henry came into his own, a settlement that would be made with measure and recourse to due process when resolving disputes, rather than one marked by ruthless dispossession of those who had been Stephen's men. There were security arrangements, too, to make sure the deal stuck when Stephen died. It was established how strategically important castles would be put into the duke's hands, or into those of his men, when Stephen was gone. The reconciliation was sealed with a kiss of peace. A progress followed, joining together king and duke in a peripatetic advertisement of love and joy in which they were newly bound. For this was the language in which a new politics was portrayed, a language of familial affection in place of strife, in which the antagonists were recast as adoptive father and son. 'Thus,' said Henry of Huntingdon,

God's mercy brought to England 'a dawn of peace after a night of misery.'[18]

It must have seemed that Stephen would now, at least, have his Indian summer. William of Newburgh imagined the king, robed at long last in legitimacy, and so able to make a progress unhindered around his realm. The threat posed by castles, for so long his bane, now melted 'as wax before a fire'.[19] The experience of uncontested authority must have been bittersweet, however, for there would be no dynasty. In the event, it was also brief. In the autumn, after meetings at Dover with the Count of Flanders, Stephen was taken ill with pains in his guts and fluxes of blood.[20] The illness seems to have come on him suddenly, but it must have become plain quickly that little could be done to save him. His wife's confessor, Ralph, Prior of Holy Trinity, Aldgate, was fetched and, in scenes the chroniclers do not trouble to describe, the king would have made a final confession, taken communion if he were able, and then waited as he was anointed, his senses sealed against a fading world. Within a year of the peace settlement Stephen was dead, breathing his last on 25 October 1154.

He had been gentle and mild, chivalrous and brave. He had pulled off the difficult trick of seizing the throne with a weak claim and he had almost made this good, too, with a display of decisive action akin to that of his uncles, William Rufus and Henry I, at the very start of his reign. Neither the fragility of his claim nor – at first – the response of his rival, Matilda, had undone him. For the cause of the empress was rejuvenated in the midst of Stephen's splintering authority. It was what Stephen did, and perhaps what Stephen was, in the years immediately after his coronation, that started this: his inability to master the many threats that grew around him; the sense of a king not entirely at ease in his own royal skin; and – perhaps even at an early date – hints of darkness in his character that found expression in mistrustfulness and flashes of malevolence. These were the circumstances that conspired in Stephen's initial undoing. What Matilda's belated advent did was to ensure that disorder then spread and intensified as an Anglo-Norman realm forged by – and for – kings who were powerful found itself divided and ruled by a king under challenge. 'Anarchy' is not a word that captures the complexity of what followed, because structures survived and much of the violence had a coherence – government did not everywhere collapse, royal authority did not everywhere disintegrate – and trouble arose among the barons not simply because ambitions were unleashed, but as a by-product of attempts to find a measure of security in a rapidly changing world. And yet for those caught up in events, many regions must often have seemed anarchic under Stephen's rule. There was unrest of a kind not seen in King Henry's England, and the shock and horror the chroniclers express – for all their capacity to moralize and exaggerate – cannot lightly be set aside. That it was the poor who often suffered most seems beyond doubt; that the wars fought around them, and sometimes in their midst, had a hidden purpose or inner logic would have been cold comfort. We cannot hear their voices, but seen through their eyes, it is unlikely that Stephen's rule could have been considered in any way a success. And for Stephen, too, it could only have been a failure. He would have sought renown, to live on in a reputation fitting for a grandson of William the Conqueror, and to live on in an exalted bloodline. He would have known, when Death came for him as he lay at Dover, that he could have neither wish. The chroniclers would not handle his memory kindly. And, though he had risen from the highest echelons of landholding society to wear the crown, his heir, William, would now fall again, taking the family name with him, back to the rank at which his father had begun.

On news reaching him of Stephen's death, Henry of Anjou did not rush, busying himself on the continent about the conclusion of a siege. None the less, even in his absence his new kingdom was still. The mechanism established in 1153 worked; the consensus the treaty articulated held, as Henry seemed to know it would. He crossed to England, eventually, on 7 December. His ship set out from Barfleur, skirting the rocks that had been the cause of so much grief. He travelled to London immediately. They welcomed him there joyously, as once they had welcomed Stephen. And on 17 December, in Westminster Abbey, Archbishop Theobald set the crown of England on a young man's head in a ritual that followed the familiar script, but this time confirming what he was already known to be, rather than making him something new.

Henry of Huntingdon delighted in this new beginning. He reached for a solar metaphor. The mortal chill, he said, was now over; the kingdom was warmed in the 'heat of a new sun'.[21] Whether love or fear of the new king disarmed those who might otherwise have resisted was not made plain by the chronicler; he did not countenance the possibility that so much fighting during Stephen's reign had altered baronial dispositions – such that magnates now stayed their hands in this moment of danger. And yet that calculation – more than love or fear – was the thing inscribed in baronial actions in the early years of King Henry's rule. For the generality of barons did not resist him. They acquiesced to his authority as he aggressively clawed back all that he thought was rightfully his – demolishing 'adulterine' castles; rolling back purprestures, encroachments on royal lands; prising local government from the tight fists of the earls.[22]

Most were at least accepting – 'the rapacious wolves fled', said William of Newburgh, 'or were turned into sheep' – but a few were not.[23] William of Aumale, established in his Yorkshire fastness, 'burned with indignation', and yet even he folded before royal power.[24] Roger of Hereford and Hugh Mortimer, men grown used to being left to their own devices, shut up castles against the king in the marches.[25] Again, both capitulated when it became plain that the king meant business. They were exceptions who proved a rule. Circumstance before Stephen's reign, and military expansionism during its course, had gifted them geographically concentrated lands that they could aspire to defend. They had less need of royal power than most, and they had better means to resist it than men whose properties were scattered. But confronted by a new king backed by a majority of barons chastened by war, and ready to rally behind him, their opposition, too, melted.

If the strengthening inner logic of Henry's claim and the

politics of landholding, rather than the providence so beloved of chroniclers, were the forces working to put the crown on Henry's head and keep it there, contingency had played its part too. Fortuna, in a final turn, cleared away rivals. Not only Eustace but also Ranulf of Chester had gone the way of all flesh. In the far north, David, King of Scots had died on 24 May 1153, a passing that had been all the more momentous because, in 1152, his son and heir, Prince Henry, had predeceased him. The succession in Scotland, as in England, was smooth; there was no tussle over the crown. But it passed to David's grandson, Malcolm, a boy of but twelve years. He was ill-fitted to resist Henry of England, who, already seeing his power stretched out over Normandy, Anjou and Aquitaine, was now resolved to recover everything that had been lost in the north.

There had been a number of possible futures on that winter's night when Henry I died in 1135, but, following Stephen's death in the autumn of 1154, in the Angevin sunshine, there seemed to be only one – one that the greater part of the elite had strained to secure. As the future's course was fixed, so the past was reimagined. Henry II's succession was the belated fulfilment of Henry I's scheme – the old king had triumphed from the grave – and it would mark a return to the good old days of his rule, the restoration of 'grandfatherly times'. Stephen's reign had been an interruption, a hiatus, almost an interregnum. The king's friends, meanwhile, laid his mortal remains to rest at Faversham, where he and his queen had endowed a monastery that they must have imagined as a dynastic mausoleum.[26] Instead, it became the graveyard of their ambitions, with Stephen interred beside the wife and son who had predeceased him. None of the chroniclers troubled to detail the king's obsequies or sketched out an obituary, as if they wished to bury his memory with his bones. Henry of Anjou's partisans can be forgiven the abbreviation, but even the *Gesta* author seems to have concluded by this point that he had written the story of a failed cause. He supplied no summation of Stephen's life; he seems not to have known the manner of his death, suggesting that a sudden fever had swept the king away, and he said nothing at all about his interment, not even where it took place.[27] He ended not with Stephen at all, leaving his readers instead with applause for a new king ringing in their ears.

Notes

My general practice, in quoting from primary sources, has been to adopt the translations used in the modern critical editions. I have sometimes slightly adjusted these and offer my own translations where otherwise unavailable.

PROLOGUE

1. Detailed accounts appear in *The Ecclesiastical History of Orderic Vitalis*, ed. and trans. M. Chibnall, 6 vols (Oxford: Oxford University Press, 1969–80), vol. 6, pp. 296–307; also *The Chronicle of John of Worcester*, vol. 3, ed. and trans. R. R. Darlington, P. McGurk and J. Bray (Oxford: Oxford University Press, 1998), pp. 146–7. For discussion, see J. A. Green, *Henry I: King of England and Duke of Normandy* (Cambridge: Cambridge University Press, 2006), pp. 164ff., which informs what follows; also C. Warren Hollister, *Henry I*, ed. and completed by Amanda Clark Frost (New Haven, Conn.: Yale University Press, 2001). On cross-Channel connections, see D. Bates, *The Normans and Empire: The Ford Lectures Delivered in the University of Oxford During Hilary Term 2010* (Oxford: Oxford University Press, 2013).
2. *Orderic Vitalis*, vol. 6, pp. 296–7.
3. According to the account given in *Orderic Vitalis*, vol. 6, pp. 298–301.
4. William of Malmesbury, *Gesta Regum Anglorum*, ed. and trans. R. A. B. Mynors, R. M. Thomson and M. Winterbottom, 2 vols (Oxford: Oxford University Press, 1998–9), vol. 1, pp. 760–61.
5. The historiography of the last three decades has tended to revise earlier accounts of 'anarchy'. For discussion see D. Crouch, *The Reign of King Stephen, 1135–1154* (Harlow: Longman, 2000), pp. 1–7. Some recent work, though careful not to reinstate older interpretations, has again argued for relatively high levels of violence during the period: H. M. Thomas, 'Violent Disorder in Stephen's England: A Maximum Argument', in *King Stephen's Reign, 1135–1154*, ed. P. Dalton and G. White (Woodbridge: Boydell & Brewer, 2008).

1. WAITING FOR THE BOMB

1. *Orderic Vitalis*, vol. 6, pp. 448–9.

2. W. M. Aird, *Robert Curthose, Duke of Normandy, c.1050–1134* (Woodbridge: Boydell & Brewer, 2011), especially chs 3 and 4; G. Garnett, 'Robert Curthose: The Duke Who Lost His Trousers', *Anglo-Norman Studies*, 35 (2013).

3. For his succession, see F. Barlow, *William Rufus* (London: Methuen, 1983), pp. 53–98; E. Mason, *William II: Rufus, the Red King* (Stroud: Tempus, 2005), pp. 46–70. For Henry's accession, see Green, *Henry I*, chs 2 and 3.

4. K. Leyser, 'The Anglo-Norman Succession, 1120–1125', *Anglo-Norman Studies*, 13 (1990).

5. M. Chibnall, *The Empress Matilda: Queen Consort, Queen Mother and Lady of the English* (Oxford: Oxford University Press, 1991), pp. 45–63; William of Malmesbury, *Historia Novella: The Contemporary History*, ed. E. King and trans K. R. Potter (Oxford: Oxford University Press, 1998), pp. 6–9.

6. *Gesta Regum Anglorum*, vol. 1, pp. 782–3.

7. Chibnall, *Empress Matilda*, pp. 50–63; for Henry's plans: J. Green, 'Henry I and the Origins of the Civil War', in *King Stephen's Reign*, ed. Dalton and White.

8. Symeon of Durham interpreted the proposed marriage as a means to stave off the threat posed by William Clito. See *Symeonis Monachis Opera Omnia*, ed. T. Arnold, Rolls Series, 2 vols (London: 1885), vol. 2, p. 282.

9. Green, *Henry I*, pp. 201–2.

10. *Orderic Vitalis*, vol. 6, pp. 466ff.

11. D. Crouch, 'Robert, First Earl of Gloucester', in *Oxford Dictionary of National Biography* (Oxford: Oxford University Press, 2004–15; hereafter *ODNB*).

12. For Adela and her family: K. LoPrete, *Adela of Blois: Countess and Lord (c.1067–1137)* (Dublin: Four Courts Press, 2007).

13. E. King, 'Stephen of Blois, Count of Mortain and Boulogne', *English Historical Review*, 115 (2000).

14. *Historia Novella*, pp. 8–9.

15. *John of Worcester*, pp. 208–11; see also *Historia Novella*, p. 22.

16. R. H. C. Davis, *King Stephen, 1135–1154*, 3rd edn (London: Longman, 1990), p. 12; for the broader problem of violence on a king's death: G. Garnett, *Conquered England: Kingship, Succession and Tenure* (Oxford: Oxford University Press, 2007), ch. 3.

17. *Orderic Vitalis*, vol. 5, pp. 292–3.

18. Succinctly put as a prelude to his main business in J. C. Holt, *Magna Carta*, 2nd edn (Cambridge: Cambridge University Press, 1992), p. 28.

19. E. Cownie, *Religious Patronage in Anglo-Norman England* (Woodbridge: Boydell & Brewer, 1998), pp. 185–296.

20. Bates, *Normans and Empire*, especially ch. 5.

21. C. Given-Wilson, *Chronicles: The Writing of History in Medieval England* (London: Hambledon, 2004); for a particularly sharp critique of chronicles as flawed sources, see D. Matthew, *King Stephen* (London: Hambledon, 2002), pp. 42ff.

22. Davis, *King Stephen*, p. 12.

23. For instance: *Orderic Vitalis*, vol. 6, pp. 434–47.

24. *Orderic Vitalis*, vol. 6, pp. 380–81.

25. *Le Livre de Sibille*, ed. H. Shields (London: Anglo-Norman Text Society, 1979), pp. 3–27; also J. Crick, 'Geoffrey of Monmouth, Prophecy and History', *Journal of Medieval History*, 18 (1992).

26. See C. Warren Hollister, 'The Aristocracy', in *The Anarchy of King Stephen's Reign*, ed. E. King (Oxford: Clarendon Press, 1994).

27. A. Murray, *Reason and Society in the Middle Ages* (Oxford: Clarendon Press, 1978), pp. 98–101.

28. For Henry's death, see Green, *Henry I*, pp. 219ff.

29. *Historia Novella*, pp. 26–7.

30. *Gesta Stephani*, ed. K. R. Potter and R. H. C. Davis (Oxford: Oxford University Press, 1976), pp. 12–13.

31. H. J. Tanner, *Families, Friends and Allies: Boulogne and Politics in Northern France and England, 879–1160* (Leiden: Brill, 2004), pp. 181–217.

32. *Historia Novella*, pp. 30–31.

33. *Gesta Stephani*, pp. 8–9.

34. For Henry, see E. King, 'Henry de Blois', *ODNB*.

35. *Orderic Vitalis*, vol. 6, pp. 58–9 (discussing Henry I and Robert Curthose); vol. 5, pp. 214–15 (considering the reign of William Rufus). The citation is of Matthew 6:24.

36. *Orderic Vitalis*, vol. 6, pp. 454–5.

37. LoPrete, *Adela*, p. 168.

38. LoPrete, *Adela*, pp. 167–8.

39. Bates, *Normans and Empire*, p. 92; Jean-Yves Tilliette, *Baudri de Bourgueil: Poèmes*, 2 vols (Paris: Belles Lettres, 1998–2002), vol. 2, no. 134; J. A. Brundage, 'An Errant Crusader: Stephen of Blois', *Traditio*, 16 (1960).

40. LoPrete, *Adela*, especially chs 4 and 6.

41. For discussion, see E. King, 'The *Gesta Stephani*', in *Writing Medieval Biography, 750–1250: Essays in Honour of Professor Frank Barlow*, ed. D. Bates, J. Crick and S. Hamilton (Woodbridge: Boydell & Brewer, 2006).

42. *Gesta Stephani*, pp. 9–15.

43. The chronicler Gervase of Canterbury, writing in the later twelfth century, alleged that the king had, on his deathbed, released his barons from their oaths. See *The Historical Works of Gervase of Canterbury*, ed. W. Stubbs, Rolls Series, 2 vols (London: 1879–80), vol. 1, p. 94. The claim also appears in the Ely narrative, *Liber Eliensis*, ed. E. O. Blake (London: Camden Society, 1962), p. 285.

44. For this characteristic interregnal violence, see Garnett, *Conquered England*, ch. 3; also Bates, *Normans and Empire*, pp. 74ff.

45. *Gesta Stephani*, pp. 3–5; C. R. Young, *The Royal Forests of Medieval England* (Leicester: Leicester University Press, 1979), pp. 7–17.

46. *John of Worcester*, pp. 216–19.

47. *Gesta Stephani*, pp. 6–7.

48. On this point, see B. Weiler, 'Kingship, Usurpation and Propaganda in Twelfth-Century Europe: The Case of Stephen', *Anglo-Norman Studies*, 28 (2000).

49. *Gesta Stephani*, pp. 12–13.

2. A FRONT OF IRON?

1. The rite was probably patterned on that used in the coronation of Henry I, for which see Green, *Henry I*, pp. 44–5; also J. L. Nelson, 'The Rites of the Conqueror', *Anglo-Norman Studies*, 4 (1982).

2. *Gesta Stephani*, pp. 10–11.

3. Matilda's case was subsequently heard at the Second Lateran Council. A spurious claim, that Matilda's mother had taken the veil and so she was not a legitimate heir, became the basis for Stephen's defence, which was prosecuted with ingenuity and ultimate success by his advocate, Arnulf of Lisieux. For which, see *The Historia Pontificalis of John of Salisbury*, ed. and trans. M. Chibnall (Oxford: Oxford University Press, 1986), pp. 83ff.

4. *John of Worcester*, pp. 198–203.

5. *Gesta Stephani*, pp. 8–9.

6. *Henry, Archdeacon of Huntingdon: Historia Anglorum*, ed. and trans. D. Greenway (Oxford: Oxford University Press, 1996), pp. 704–5.

7. *Gesta Stephani*, pp. 12–13.

8. *Orderic Vitalis*, vol. 5, pp. 296–7; also pp. 316–17.

9. J. Green, 'Henry I and the North of England', *Transactions of the Royal Historical Society*, 6th Series, 17 (2007).

10. On David: R. Oram, *David I: The King Who Made Scotland* (Stroud: Tempus, 2008), pp. 49–72; G. W. S. Barrow, *David I of Scotland (1124–1153): The Balance of New and Old* (Reading: University of Reading, 1985).

11. *Gesta Stephani*, pp. 54–5; for the point about 'modernization', see the outline in D. A. Carpenter, *The Struggle for Mastery in Britain 1066–1284* (Oxford: Oxford University Press, 2003), pp. 178–86; also G. W. S. Barrow, *The Anglo-Norman Era in Scottish History* (Oxford: Oxford University Press, 1980); K. J. Stringer, 'State-Building in Twelfth-Century Britain: David I, King of Scots, and Northern England', in *Government, Religion and Society in Northern England 1000–1700*, ed. J. C. Appleby and P. Dalton (Stroud: Sutton, 1997).

12. On David's ambitions, see K. J. Stringer, *The Reign of Stephen: Kingship, Warfare and Government in the Twelfth Century* (London: Routledge, 1993), pp. 28–37; Oram, *David I*, ch. 8 and especially ch. 10.

13. *Gesta Stephani*, pp. 54–5.

14. H. R. T. Summerson, *Medieval Carlisle: The City and the Borders from the Late Eleventh to the Mid-Sixteenth Century*, 2 vols (Kendal: Cumberland and Westmorland Antiquarian and Archaeological Society, 1993), vol. 1, ch. 1; C. Phythian-Adams, *Land of the Cumbrians: A Study of British Provincial Origins, AD 400–1120* (Aldershot: Scolar Press, 1996), ch. 2.

15. W. E. Kapelle, *The Norman Conquest of the North: The Region and Its Transformation, 1000–1135* (London: Croom Helm, 1979), pp. 191–230; D. W. Rollason, *Northumbria, 500–1100: Creation and Destruction of a Kingdom* (Cambridge: Cambridge University Press, 2003), especially chs 6 and 7.

16. For further discussion, see E. King, *King Stephen* (New Haven, Conn.: Yale University Press, 2010), pp. 53–4.

17. Again, see King, *Stephen*, pp. 50–51, 60–61.

18. R. R. Davies, *Conquest, Co-existence and Change: Wales 1063–1415* (Oxford: Oxford University Press, 1987), ch. 4; D. Crouch, 'The March and the Welsh Kings', in *Anarchy of Stephen's Reign*, ed. King; Crouch, *King Stephen*, ch. 3.

19. *Orderic Vitalis*, vol. 6, pp. 442–5.

20. *Giraldi Cambrensis Opera*, vol. 6, ed. J. F. Dimock, Rolls Series (London: 1868), pp. 87–9.

21. *John of Worcester*, pp. 218–19.

22. *John of Worcester*, pp. 220–21.

23. R. Bearman, 'Baldwin de Redvers: Some Aspects of a Baronial Career in the Reign of King Stephen', *Anglo-Norman Studies*, 18 (1996).

24. *Gesta Stephani*, pp. 32–3.

25. *Gesta Stephani*, pp. 40–41.

26. *Historia Anglorum*, pp. 706–9.

27. Aird, *Robert Curthose*, pp. 115–17, for Rufus yielding to advice to be merciful.

28. *Orderic Vitalis*, vol. 6, pp. 450–51, 470ff.; M. Chibnall, *The World of Orderic Vitalis: Norman Monks and Norman Knights* (Oxford: Oxford University Press, 1964), pp. 17–27, 40–41.

29. *Orderic Vitalis*, vol. 5, pp. 300–301; for the difficulties of ruling the duchy, see Aird, *Robert Curthose*, ch. 4; for lucid discussion of complex power politics: D. Power, *Norman Frontier in the Twelfth and Thirteenth Centuries* (Cambridge: Cambridge University Press, 2004), chs 9–11.

30. *Orderic Vitalis*, vol. 6, pp. 480ff.

31. *Orderic Vitalis*, vol. 6, pp. 494–5ff.

32. Crouch, 'March and the Welsh Kings', in *Anarchy of Stephen's Reign*, ed. King; Crouch, *King Stephen*, ch. 3.

33. *Historia Novella*, pp. 32–3, 40–43.

34. *Gesta Stephani*, pp. 68–9.

35. *Historia Novella*, pp. 40–41.

36. *Historia Anglorum*, pp. 712–13.

37. *Historia Anglorum*, pp. 756–7.

38. On this point about the problem posed by castles, see Stringer, *Reign of Stephen*, pp. 15–16 and pp. 16–17 (on Stephen's tactics in light of this).

39. *Gesta Stephani*, pp. 34–5.

40. *Orderic Vitalis*, vol. 6, pp. 60–63. He was putting words in the mouth of Bishop Serlo of Sées (d. 1123), who, although discussing Robert Curthose, was giving voice to a general principle.

41. *Gesta Stephani*, pp. 14–15; *John of Worcester*, pp. 242–3; *Historia Anglorum*, pp. 706–7.

42. *Historia Novella*, pp. 32–3.

43. *Gesta Stephani*, pp. 22–3.

44. *Historia Anglorum*, pp. 732–3; *Gesta Stephani*, pp. 10–11; *Gesta Regum Anglorum*, vol. 1, pp. 700–701.

45. For example: *Historia Anglorum*, pp. 706–9; *Historia Novella*, pp. 28–9.

46. *John of Worcester*, pp. 248–51; *Orderic Vitalis*, vol. 6, pp. 520–23.

47. *Gesta Stephani*, pp. 50–51.

48. *Historia Anglorum*, pp. 710–11; M. Strickland, 'Securing the North: Invasion and the Strategy of Defence in Twelfth-Century Anglo-Scottish Warfare', *Anglo-Norman Studies*, 12 (1990).

49. D. Nicholl, *Thurstan Archbishop of York (1114–40)* (York: Stonegate Press, 1964), pp. 221–32.

50. P. Dalton, 'Eustace Fitz John and the Politics of Anglo-Norman England: The Rise and Survival of a Twelfth-Century Royal Servant', *Speculum*, 71 (1996).
51. *Gesta Stephani*, pp. 50–53; the biblical reference is Daniel 5:5.
52. John of Hexham, *Symeonis Historia Regum Continuata per Johannem Hagustal-densem*, in *Symeonis Monachi Opera Omnia*, vol. 2, ed. T. Arnold, Rolls Series (London: 1885), pp. 289–90, 330–31; also for David's protection of Hexham, see Richard of Hexham, *De Gestis Regis Stephani et De Bello Standardo*, in *Chronicles of the Reigns of Stephen, Henry II and Richard I*, ed. R. Howlett, Rolls Series, 4 vols (London: 1884–9), vol. 3, pp. 153–4.
53. William of Newburgh, *Historia Rerum Anglicarum*, in *Chronicles of the Reigns of Stephen, Henry II and Richard I*, ed. Howlett, vol. 1, p. 72; William of Malmesbury pronounced that David's time in the Norman court 'had rubbed off all the barbarian gaucherie of Scottish manners', in *Gesta Regum Anglorum*, vol. 1, pp. 726–7.
54. *Historia Anglorum*, pp. 726–7.

3. FICKLE FORTUNA

1. G. J. White, *Restoration and Reform, 1153–1165* (Cambridge: Cambridge University Press, 2000), pp. 12–76, where there is also a positive interpretation of the durability of government structures.
2. *Historia Novella*, pp. 46–51; *Gesta Stephani*, pp. 72–5; *Historia Anglorum*, pp. 718–21; S. Marritt, 'Stephen and the Bishops', *Anglo-Norman Studies*, 24 (2001).
3. *Gesta Stephani*, pp. 96–7; *Historia Novella*, p. 65.
4. D. Crouch, *The Beaumont Twins: The Roots and Branches of Power in the Twelfth Century* (Cambridge: 1986), pp. 38–45; see also discussion in K. Yoshitake, 'The Arrest of the Bishops and Its Consequences', *Journal of Medieval History*, 14 (1988).
5. *Historia Novella*, pp. 46–7; and for this suggestion about motivation, see King, *Stephen*, pp. 108–11.
6. *Gesta Stephani*, pp. 74–5.
7. K. Yoshitake, 'The Exchequer in the Reign of Stephen', *English Historical Review*, 103 (1988); J. A. Green, 'Financing Stephen's War', *Anglo-Norman Studies*, 14 (1992).
8. Walter Map, *De Nugis Curialium: Courtiers' Trifles*, ed. and trans. M. R. James, rev. R. A. B. Mynors and C. N. L. Brooke (Oxford: Clarendon Press, 1983), pp. 474–5.
9. *Orderic Vitalis*, vol. 6, pp. 534–5.
10. *John of Worcester*, pp. 252–3.
11. *Historia Anglorum*, pp. 724–5.
12. For the detail, see King, *Stephen*, pp. 145–8; also P. Dalton, 'In Neutro Latere: The Armed Neutrality of Ranulf II, Earl of Chester', *Anglo-Norman Studies*, 14 (1991).
13. *Gesta Stephani*, pp. 110–13; *Historia Anglorum*, pp. 732–3.
14. *Historia Anglorum*, pp. 734–5.
15. *Historia Novella*, pp. 86–7.
16. *Historia Anglorum*, 738–9.
17. Ibid.
18. *Historia Novella*, pp. 90–97.

19. *Historia Novella*, pp. 91ff.

20. H. J. Tanner, 'Queenship: Office, Custom or Ad Hoc? The Case of Queen Matilda III of England (1135–52)', in *Eleanor of Aquitaine: Lord and Lady*, ed. B. Wheeler and J. Carmi Parsons (Basingstoke: Palgrave, 2008).

21. See *Gesta Stephani*, pp. 116ff.; *Historia Novella*, pp. 98–9; *Historia Anglorum*, pp. 738–9; also for events from the perspective of the empress, H. Castor, *She-Wolves: The Women Who Ruled England before Elizabeth* (London: Faber & Faber, 2010), ch. 3; Chibnall, *Empress Matilda*, ch. 5.

22. *Gesta Stephani*, pp. 118–19.

23. For chronicle representations of (aristocratic) women, see S. M. Johns, *Noblewomen, Aristocracy and Power in the Twelfth-Century Anglo-Norman Realm* (Manchester: Manchester University Press, 2003), pp. 13–29.

24. *Gesta Stephani*, pp. 126–7.

25. *Symeonis Historia*, pp. 309–10.

26. *Historia Novella*, pp. 99ff.

27. *John of Worcester*, pp. 300–303; *Gesta Stephani*, pp. 126–37, especially pp. 132–5.

28. *Liber Eliensis*, ed. Blake, p. 323; *Orderic Vitalis*, vol. 6, pp. 548–9; for a (qualified) view of the contraction of royal authority, see G. J. White, 'Continuity in Government', in *Anarchy of Stephen's Reign*, ed. King, especially pp. 130–35.

29. For the early example of William of Aumale, see P. Dalton, *Conquest, Anarchy and Lordship: Yorkshire 1066–1154* (Cambridge: Cambridge University Press, 1994), pp. 152–95; White, *Restoration and Reform*, pp. 57–67.

30. J. A. Green, *Government of England Under Henry I* (Cambridge: Cambridge University Press, 1986), pp. 51–94.

31. M. Blackburn, 'Coinage and Currency', in *Anarchy of Stephen's Reign*, ed. King; M. Allen, *Mints and Money in Medieval England* (Cambridge: Cambridge University Press, 2012), ch. 1.

32. Initially, Stephen's image was preserved on these issues, but from the early 1140s this changes.

33. *Historia Rerum Anglicarum*, pp. 69–70.

34. Dalton, *Conquest, Anarchy and Lordship*, pp. 178–95; P. Dalton, 'Aiming at the Impossible: Ranulf II, Earl of Chester and Lincolnshire in the Reign of Stephen', in *The Earldom of Chester and Its Charters*, ed. A. T. Thacker (Chester: Chester Archaeological Society, 1991); E. King, 'Dispute Settlement in Anglo-Norman England', *Anglo-Norman Studies*, 14 (1992).

35. *Historia Rerum Anglicarum*, pp. 69–70.

4. THE TRACKLESS MAZE

1. *Historia Anglorum*, pp. 742–3; for a vivid sketch of the escape: *The History of the Norman People: Wace's Roman de Rou*, trans. G. S. Burgess (Woodbridge: Boydell & Brewer, 2004), p. 5.

2. *Gesta Stephani*, pp. 140–45.

3. Crouch, *King Stephen*, pp. 206–8.

4. *Historia Novella*, pp. 80–81. For this issue: S. Bagge, 'Ethics, Politics and Providence in William of Malmesbury's *Historia Novella*', *Viator*, 41 (2010); R. M. Thomson, 'Satire, Irony and Humour in William of Malmesbury', in *Rhetoric and Renewal in*

the Latin West, 1100–1540: Essays in Honour of John O. Ward, ed. C. J. Mews, C. J. Nederman and R. M. Thomson (Turnhout: Brepols, 2003), p. 125.

5. *Gesta Stephani*, pp. 150–51, 154–5, 212–13.

6. *Gesta Stephani*, pp. 148–51.

7. See Dalton, 'Armed Neutrality', pp. 58–9.

8. *Gesta Stephani*, pp. 160ff.; *The Book of the Foundation of Walden Monastery*, ed. L. Watkiss and D. Greenway (Oxford: Oxford University Press, 1999), pp. 12–21; *Chronicon Abbatiae Ramesiensis*, ed. W. Dunn Macray, Rolls Series (London: 1886), pp. 331–2; *Historia Anglorum*, pp. 742–7; J. H. Round, *Geoffrey de Mandeville: A Study of the Anarchy* (London: Longmans, Green, 1892); R. H. C. Davis, 'Geoffrey de Mandeville Reconsidered', *English Historical Review*, 79 (1964), pp. 299–307; J. O. Prestwich, 'The Treason of Geoffrey de Mandeville', *English Historical Review*, 103 (1988).

9. *Gesta Stephani*, pp. 164–6.

10. *Walden Monastery*, ed. and trans. Greenway and Watkiss, pp. 16–19; a different, but no more flattering account appears in *Chronicon Abbatiae Ramesiensis*, ed. W. Dunn Macray, Rolls Series (London: 1886), pp. 331–2.

11. *The Peterborough Chronicle*, trans. H. A. Rositzke (New York: Columbia University Press, 1951), p. 158.

12. H. J. Thomas, 'Miracle Stories and Violence in Stephen's Reign', *Historical Society Journal*, 13 (2004).

13. *John of Worcester*, pp. 272–3.

14. *John of Worcester*, pp. 276–7.

15. *Gesta, Stephani*, pp. 112–13; *Historia Anglorum*, pp. 738–9.

16. For a particular manifestation, see T. N. Bisson, 'The Lure of Stephen's England: *Tenserie*, Flemings and a Crisis of Circumstance', in *King Stephen's Reign*, ed. Dalton and White.

17. M. Strickland, *War and Chivalry: The Conduct and Perception of War in England and Normandy, 1066–1217* (Cambridge: Cambridge University Press, 1996), pp. 258–90.

18. *Gesta Stephani*, pp. 218–21.

19. *Gesta Stephani*, pp. 134–5.

20. *De Nugis Curialium*, ed. James, pp. 474–5.

21. C. Holdsworth, 'The Church', in *Anarchy of Stephen's Reign*, ed. King, pp. 207–12.

22. *Gesta Stephani*, pp. 148–9.

23. M. Chibnall, 'Normandy', in *Anarchy of Stephen's Reign*, ed. King, pp. 102–15.

5. THE SHADOW OF THE FUTURE

1. For the young Henry: W. L. Warren, *Henry II* (London, 1973), pp. 12–53. The title of this chapter borrows Robert Axelrod's phrase, via Paul Hyams, who invokes it in his analysis of medieval conflict and co-operation in P. Hyams, *Rancor and Reconciliation in Medieval England* (Ithaca: Cornell University Press, 2003), pp. 16–21.

2. G. White, 'Ranulf (II), Earl of Chester', in *ODNB*.

3. For another view of Carlisle's importance to Ranulf, see Dalton, 'Armed Neutrality', p. 43.

4. Oram, *David I*, pp. 154–6, 188–9; Stringer, 'State-Building in Twelfth-Century Britain', pp. 57–61.

5. Events are recounted in outline in *Symeonis Historia*, p. 323.

6. King, *Stephen*, pp. 259–61; the consensus for the date of this treaty is now nearer to 1148 than 1153, which was hitherto the established range of possibilities.

7. P. Dalton, 'Churchmen and the Promotion of Peace in King Stephen's Reign', *Viator*, 31 (2000); P. Dalton, 'Civil War and Ecclesiastical Peace in the Reign of Stephen', in *War and Society in the Middle Ages*, ed. D. Dunn (Liverpool: Liverpool University Press, 2000).

8. Crouch, *King Stephen*, pp. 245–7.

9. A. Saltman, *Theobald Archbishop of Canterbury* (London: Athlone Press, 1956), pp. 36–9.

10. Raymond of Marseilles had dedicated a treatise on the astrolabe to Robert, Earl of Leicester in *c.*1140; likewise Adelard of Bath dedicated one to Henry of Anjou in the mid or late 1140s. See J. D. North, 'Some Norman Horoscopes', in *Adelard of Bath: An English Scientist and Arabist of the Early Twelfth Century*, ed. C. Burnett (London: Warburg Institute, 1987).

11. Warren, *Henry II*, pp. 46–8; R. V. Turner, *Eleanor of Aquitaine: Queen of France, Queen of England* (New Haven, Conn.: Yale University Press, 2009), pp. 100–112.

12. *Gesta Stephani*, pp. 214–15, 222–5; but for suggestions that the *Gesta* author's position was in fact more consistent than it seems, see E. King, 'The *Gesta Stephani*'.

13. *Historia Anglorum*, pp. 764–5.

14. *Gesta Stephani*, pp. 238–9.

15. *Historia Anglorum*, pp. 766–7.

16. *Gesta Stephani*, pp. 238–9.

17. *Gervase of Canterbury*, ed. Stubbs, vol. 1, p. 56; for the resultant treaty, see J. C. Holt, '1153: The Treaty of Winchester', in *Anarchy of Stephen's Reign*, ed. King.

18. *Historia Anglorum*, pp. 770–71.

19. *Historia Rerum Anglicarum*, p. 94.

20. *Gervase of Canterbury*, ed. Stubbs, vol. 1, p. 159.

21. *Historia Anglorum*, pp. 776–7.

22. E. Amt, *The Accession of Henry II in England: Royal Government Restored, 1149–1159* (Woodbridge: Boydell & Brewer, 1993); White, *Restoration and Reform*, especially chs 3 and 4; E. King, 'The Accession of Henry II', in *Henry II : New Interpretations*, ed. C. Harper-Bill and N. Vincent (Woodbridge: Boydell & Brewer, 2007).

23. *Historia Rerum Anglicarum*, p. 102.

24. *Historia Rerum Anglicarum*, pp. 103–5; see also Dalton, *Conquest, Anarchy and Lordship*, p. 176, though he also stresses the relatively generous terms offered by Henry to the earl.

25. *Historia Rerum Anglicarum*, p. 105.

26. Briefly noted in *Historia Anglorum*, pp. 774–5.

27. *Gesta Stephani*, pp. 240–41.

Further Reading

Many historians have been intrigued by what went 'wrong' during Stephen's reign and by the question of just how wrong things went, in terms of the violence and dislocation emphasized by the chroniclers. Important and comprehensive studies are E. King, *King Stephen* (New Haven, Conn.: Yale University Press, 2010), and D. Crouch, *The Reign of King Stephen, 1135–1154* (Harlow: Longman, 2000). There is also brief but incisive discussion in K. J. Stringer, *The Reign of Stephen: Kingship, Warfare and Government in the Twelfth Century* (London: Routledge, 1993). Classic studies, still of value, are R. H. C. Davis, *King Stephen, 1135–1154*, 3rd edn (London: Longman, 1990), and H. A. Cronne, *The Reign of Stephen: Anarchy in England* (London: Weidenfeld & Nicolson, 1970). Beyond the biographies, a major recent monograph puts the reign in the context of developing Norman power: G. Garnett, *Conquered England: Kingship, Succession and Tenure* (Oxford: Oxford University Press, 2007). The prelude to Stephen's rule is traced expertly in J. A. Green, *Henry I: King of England and Duke of Normandy* (Cambridge: Cambridge University Press, 2006). And for Stephen's family, see K. LoPrete, *Adela of Blois: Countess and Lord (c.1067–1137)* (Dublin: Four Courts Press, 2007). The empress is treated in a fine study, M. Chibnall, *The Empress Matilda: Queen Consort, Queen Mother and Lady of the English* (Oxford: Oxford University Press, 1991), and there is an account at once vivid and persuasive in its rescue of Matilda from hostile contemporary reportage: H. Castor, *She-Wolves: The Women Who Ruled England Before Elizabeth* (London: Faber & Faber, 2010). For her son, Henry of Anjou, a good starting point remains W. L. Warren, *Henry II* (London: Methuen, 1973).

Stephen's northern nemesis, David I of Scotland, has a lower profile in popular historiography than he deserves, but there is an accessible biographical treatment in R. Oram, *David I: The King Who Made Scotland* (Stroud: Tempus, 2008), and aspects of his rule are traced in G. W. S. Barrow, *David I of Scotland (1124–1153): The Balance of New and Old* (Reading: University of Reading, 1985). For his ambitions in the north of England, see K. J. Stringer, 'State-Building in Twelfth-Century Britain: David I, King of Scots, and Northern England', in *Government, Religion and Society in Northern England 1000–1700*, edited by J. C. Appleby and P. Dalton (Stroud: Sutton, 1997). The consolidation of Norman power in northern England was treated by W. E. Kapelle, *The Norman Conquest of the North: The Region and Its Transformation, 1000–1135* (London: Croom Helm, 1979), although a number of his arguments have been called into question. For Yorkshire there is the excellent P. Dalton, *Conquest, Anarchy and Lordship: Yorkshire 1066–1154* (Cambridge: Cambridge University Press, 1994).

Many aspects of the reign are explored in two important collections of essays: *The Anarchy of King Stephen's Reign*, edited by E. King (Oxford: Oxford University Press, 1994), and *King Stephen's Reign, 1135–1154*, edited by P. Dalton and G. White (Woodbridge: Boydell & Brewer, 2008). Additionally, for finance see J. Green, 'Financing Stephen's War', *Anglo-Norman Studies*, 14 (1991). For the Norman elite generally, see J. A. Green, *The Aristocracy of Norman England* (Cambridge: Cambridge University Press, 1997). Waleran and Robert de Beaumont, important in their own right and also as exemplars of aristocratic behaviour, are considered in D. Crouch, *The Beaumont Twins: The Roots and Branches of Power in the Twelfth Century* (Cambridge: Cambridge University Press, 1986). Many of the other important players have received excellent brief treatments in the *Oxford Dictionary of National Biography* (Oxford: Oxford University Press, 2004–15). See especially D. Crouch, 'Robert, First Earl of Gloucester'; B. R. Kemp, 'Roger of Salisbury (d. 1139)'; C. Warren

Hollister, 'Geoffrey de Mandeville, First Earl of Essex'; G. White, 'Ranulf II [Ranulf de Gernon], Fourth Earl of Chester (d. 1153)'. Military strategy and aristocratic values are examined in M. Strickland, *War and Chivalry: The Conduct and Perception of War in England and Normandy, 1066–1217* (Cambridge: Cambridge University Press, 1996).

It is also possible to explore Stephen's reign through contemporary narratives, many of which exist in modern editions and translations. The reign in its entirety is recounted in *Gesta Stephani*, edited by K. R. Potter and R. H. C. Davis (Oxford: Oxford University Press, 1976), though the account becomes thinner for the 1140s and early 1150s. Henry of Huntingdon is an important witness to the later years: *Henry, Archdeacon of Huntingdon, Historia Anglorum*, edited and translated by D. Greenway (Oxford: Oxford University Press, 1996). The chronicle record of Stephen's early rule is richer. The principal authorities, beyond *Gesta Stephani*, are William of Malmesbury, for which see *Historia Novella: The Contemporary History*, edited by E. King and translated by K. R. Potter (Oxford: Oxford University Press, 1998), and John of Worcester: *The Chronicle of John of Worcester*, volume 3, edited and translated by R. R. Darlington, P. McGurk and J. Bray (Oxford: Oxford University Press, 1998). Events in Normandy are described in greater detail by Orderic Vitalis, who also reflects on English politics too. See *The Ecclesiastical History of Orderic Vitalis*, volume 6, edited and translated by M. Chibnall (Oxford: Oxford University Press, 1978).

Picture Credits

1. Three ranks of knights. Pierpont Morgan Library M.736, folio 7v (Pierpont Morgan Library/Art Resource/Scala, Florence)
2. The tragedy of the *White Ship* recalled in a twelfth-century manuscript of John of Worcester's chronicle (© Corpus Christi College, Oxford, UK/Bridgeman Images)
3. Coronation of Stephen from a mid-thirteenth-century manuscript of the *Flores Historiarum* of Matthew Paris. Chetham's Library/ Bridgeman Art Library, Manchester, MS 6712 (A6.89), folio 133r (© Chetham's Library, Manchester, UK)
4. Silver coins with portraits of King William II, 'Rufus', Henry I and Stephen of Blois (akg-images/Interfoto/Friedrich)
5. The struggle for Lincoln in 1141 from a manuscript of Matthew Paris's *Chronica Maiora* of the thirteenth century. Corpus Christi College, Cambridge, MS 16, folio 55 (The Master and Fellows of Corpus Christi College, Cambridge)
6. An illustration of the Battle of Lincoln, 1141, in a manuscript of Henry of Huntingdon's chronicle, from *c.*1200. British Library Arundel MS 48, folio 168v (© The Library Board)
7. Empress Matilda at the feast celebrating her marriage to Henry V of Germany. Corpus Christi College, Cambridge, MS 373, folio 95v (The Master and Fellows of Corpus Christi College, Cambridge)
8. Furness Abbey (© David Lyons/Alamy)
9. The aftermath of the siege of Shrewsbury from a manuscript of Matthew Paris's *Chronica Maiora* of the thirteenth century. Corpus Christi College, Cambridge, MS 16, folio 64r (The Master and Fellows of Corpus Christi College, Cambridge)

10. Hell mouth and fate of the damned, Lincoln Cathedral west front (© miscellany/Alamy)

11. King Stephen depicted as a falconer, from the Anglo-Norman rhyming chronicle of Peter Langtoft. British Library MS Royal 20, A.II, folio 219v (akg-images/British Library)

Index

25/11